DIANNE'S BLESSINGS

Jim Sizemore

ISBN: 978-1-6827-3887-0 (printed edition)
Published by: Marie Marie and Leigh Publishing

Do not remember me in grief for I will remember you with love. Pray for the Angelic souls among us living ordinary lives in an extraordinary way sharing Christ's love on earth and in heaven.

This book is dedicated to Julie and Annie.

Dianne's Blessings

Contents

Dianne's Blessings

Foreword
Turner Gill

This is a story about faith. Jim and Dianne Sizemore were the first people we met when we moved into our neighborhood in Lincoln, Nebraska. Throughout the next twenty-two years, we became much more than just neighbors. We had a card club that met once or twice a week. Jim and I enjoyed golfing. He also enjoyed putting his Husker flags on his car and driving me to the stadium on Saturdays when I coached. Dianne and my wife Gayle served food at the Matt Talbot soup kitchen. They also had playdates with our youngest daughter, Margaux, and her nephew, Tyler, who were born just three months apart. Dianne and their two daughters, Julie and Annie, went to bowl games with us while Jim stayed back to work. Julie and Annie were also babysitters for our two daughters, Jordan and Margaux, and between the two of them, we rarely had to get other sitters for most of our time in Lincoln. Once we left Lincoln, Jim and Dianne came to at least one game wherever we landed—Green Bay, Buffalo, Kansas, and Virginia. We also traveled with them in order to keep the relationship going. Jim and I checked several golf courses off our bucket lists while Gayle and Dianne sat at the pools and read or went shopping. Cards were always played at night. It has always been a relaxed and enjoyable relationship that all of us have cherished.

Dianne was a lifelong Catholic, while Jim joined the Catholic Church later in life. Gayle and I are evangelical Christians. The fact that we worshipped differently never interfered with our friendship. We knew that the center of all of our beliefs was Christ, and we found a lot of joy watching Jim and Dianne grow in their faith and in their love of Christ through a most difficult journey. This book is about that journey.

God gives us all a purpose for our lives. Dianne was always a very private person who served others, remained humble in doing so, and kept her emotions close to her heart. As God revealed His purpose for her, she kept on serving, but she came out of her comfort level in order to comfort others and to allow them to comfort her in return. I think this is something that we all have to learn as Christians. It seems easier for us to want to use our gifts to give to others, but our strength is really in the times when we allow others to use their gifts for us, to be able to give others the pleasure of serving and growing in their faith. Dianne was such a great example of this. Her service to others really came full circle in her life. The joy she brought her family and friends was the same joy that she received from all of them at the end of her life.

There are so many lessons we can learn from this book and from the life of Dianne Sizemore. Dianne made a friend of everyone she met, she drew people close to her, and she gave us all a blueprint of how to live and how to die. Her love and service to others came back many fold as she endured a devastating illness the last few years of her life. While it seems that most of us feel sad or uncomfortable about people getting ready to leave this earth, so many people got to experience a celebration with Dianne as she prepared for heaven. People gathered around her for hours upon hours, days upon days, not wanting to leave, not wanting to say goodbye. I picture Christ looking down with great joy at the picture of Dianne surrounded by those she served and enjoyed, now serving and enjoying her.

I hope that everyone who reads this story of faith will learn to celebrate with their family and friends, no matter how difficult the words or actions are to share. We are honored to count ourselves among the many friends of Dianne Sizemore. And we are thrilled to support Jim in his journey of helping others learn how to live, how to die, and how to communicate with our friends, our families, and our spouses during life's most difficult journeys.

Turner Gill
July 2016

Introduction

Be strong and of good courage; be not afraid; be not frightened; or be dismayed for God is with thee wherever you go. (Joshua 1:9)

This is a story of love: God's love, Christ's love, and Dianne's love for everyone she knew and served. This is a story of the love for Dianne by her family and friends, and me. Dianne lived to serve God by serving others. By her acts of love and support of people suffering and because of her own challenge with multiple occurrences of cancer, she showed us all how to nail our suffering to Christ's cross and let him carry the burden while we embrace of joy of life. We are blessed for Dianne touching our lives and teaching us overcome our burdens and love the life we live.

This is a story of how Christ can help us face our fears and find hope. Dianne gave us more days of joy and happiness because of her faith and optimistic soul. Even when she learned she would have cancer the rest of her life, her hope grew stronger. She showed us that prayer and faith will add days to our lives. She also believed that worry and sadness will shorten our lives. Dianne would often say to relax and trust in God.

This is a story of an ordinary Catholic that lived an extraordinary life. Dianne Marie Smollen Sizemore celebrated life from October 13, 1957 until December 31, 2015. Dianne's life was full of receiving God's love and sharing her bounty through charity and compassion. Dianne's life included cancer three times during her last seven years. Dianne learned she had breast cancer in 2009. She learned the cancer returned in 2013 and again in 2014. She lived longer than any medical diagnosis predicted because of her faith, love, joy, and happiness. Dianne now has eternal joy and happiness in heaven, but she left so much on earth. Although she faced the challenges and suffering of cancer, her charity and compassion continued to grow.

Dianne's valley of darkness was full of fear early in her journey because of the unknown and continuous changing cycle of cancer and treatment. Fear pushes us to not trust in our faith and love. Fear also causes us not to know what to do with our pain. During Dianne's early years of cancer her fears led to normal reactions. What makes Dianne's journey extraordinary happened during the last two years when her suffering was the worst, when she learned that she would always have cancer. What makes her journey inspirational is that she changed her focus to comforting others as a way of increasing her hope and facing her challenges. Dianne was angelic in the way she showed us our capacity to endure suffering is greatest when we trust God.

Dianne believed Christ would help us find joy and happiness by continuing to serve others while struggling with major illness. Dianne's journey is an example for all that through pain and suffering she still was able to show her generosity and support of her Catholic faith and the people and causes important to her.

Dianne always believed in miracles and that maybe God's plan for her would include a miracle cure. Her optimistic approach to a faith-filled life helped everyone to believe in miracles. Although Dianne didn't receive her miracle cure, her inspiration to others became her miracle. Dianne taught us how we can overcome our fears of dying by continuing sharing Christ's love.

Her cancer journey inspires many who witnessed her resolve to celebrate every day as a miracle and to focus on others and not ourselves. Dianne could change sadness to joy with a simple smile and a reminder of Christ's love. She often told us to share joy and happiness and not sympathy and grief.

Dianne loved life. She believed her rewards on earth were family and friends and acts of love for strangers. Her soul was so beautiful for carrying the cross for others. Everyone could see the grace of God's work in Dianne. Dianne was closest to heaven during this time and shared Christ's love with everyone.

Dianne did not want to die, nor did she ever talk about dying. She always found the strength in her spirit to help us in our sorrow even after she passed away.

This is not a biography of Dianne's life but reflections on Dianne's journey, an inside perspective on her faith. This is also not a clinical accounting of cancer and treatments, because cancer did not define her life. This is a story of the right and wrong things we learned during the journey. I am sharing our experiences and the lessons we learned. I pray this provides comfort and guidance for anyone experiencing or starting on a similar journey. Dianne's story also shares lessons on how to share your love with someone facing life's difficult challenges.

I prayed for Christ's help to share Dianne's journey. I was also inspired by the comforting words from family and friends. I was also surprised how I would hear a verse, a prayer, or a homily that triggered me to understand what I need to write. I smiled because I knew it was Christ showing me the way. Dianne's journey is too important and is a story that needs to be told.

My facts may be blurred, but our experiences are real. So often when I share Dianne's story I can see how her faith and experiences apply to understanding her story.

Each day people we love begin a similar journey and need our prayers and love. I pray for you knowing that God has a loving plan for each of us. I know that anyone whose journey includes breast cancer that God's plan for Dianne is not the same for everyone. Her burden was rare. God's plan will be journeys for people who will overcome their burden and live daily to inspire others. I pray that as you read this story you are able to reflect on your loved one with the same reflections and find comfort in Dianne's journey. I also pray that you find Dianne's journey an inspiration for helping others with their burdens.

This story begins with a quick bio on Dianne. The chapters on "Journey with Cancer" share what happened and what we experienced. The next three chapters are reflections on how "Faith, Family, Friends, and Caregiving." "Five Conversations with Dianne" shares what I have learned since Dianne passed away and how you can change the experience for your loved ones.

I love Dianne. I miss her every day. But I smile and am filled with joy knowing her angelic approach blessed so many people in a positive way. I pray that as you read her story you also will be full of joy and happiness.

Dianne's journey was better because of so many family and friends. These acts of love are personal between Dianne and each person, and so I respect their privacy by not using their names in telling her story.

Dianne—A Vision of a Beautiful Angel

When a hand reaches out to help, I see Dianne
Comforting to the sick
Helping feed the hungry
Giving others more than they need
Finding the best in everyone

When I hear laughter, I see her beautiful face
Smile of love for every soul
Eyes full of hope and compassion
Ears for listening to the needs of others

When I cry, I feel her loving hug
Gratitude for every moment
Joy of family and friends
Serving others before ourselves
Peace for my soul

When I pray, I see her angelic nature
Faith reminding us of Christ's love
Dignity from God's Grace
Mercy and Forgiveness
When I need love, I think of Dianne.

Dianne's Blessings

A Quick Bio on Dianne

A perspective on Dianne:

Background

Dianne Marie Smollen was born in Red Granite, Wisconsin on October 13, 1958. She was the third of six children blessing her parents, Al and Maureen. She moved to Grand Island, Nebraska early in her childhood, growing up attending Catholic schools and graduating from Grand Island Central Catholic High School in Grand Island, Nebraska. Her stories of her childhood included many cousins and friends whose friendships she still cherished throughout her life.

Dianne attended University of Nebraska, making lifelong friends with everyone she met. She worked a part-time job at a bank where we met. Our first date was on August 13, 1978. We quickly knew that God had a plan for both us and decided to marry by October. We were married on January 20, 1979 just after I completed my degree. We both worked full time at the bank and were blessed with our first daughter, Julie Marie, in December 1979. Dianne decided to stay at home and raise her children rather than working. This decision also provided her time for charity work. We were again blessed in September 1982 with our second daughter, Annie Leigh.

Faith

Dianne believed in Christ as her savior. She was a devout Catholic. Faith was always the major part of her life and provided her guidance. Each time she faced a new challenge she turned to her faith for comfort and guidance.

Family

Dianne's family includes two beautiful daughters, Julie Marie and Annie Leigh. Julie is married to Charles Bolden II and has beautiful children named Holly, Charles Bolden III (Trey), and Tayia. Dianne's brothers and sisters include Mike, Theresa, Karen, Gary, and John. Each was very special to Dianne, and she was very special to them. Dianne's parents are a great example of God's plan for marriage and family and raised Dianne with love and laughter her entire life. Dianne's family included many nieces and nephews who she adored and loved to be with all the time. Dianne was always the favorite aunt and loved playing that role. Dianne loved being the aunt who goes to all the events, especially the sporting events.

Dianne's love shined most when talking about her family. She was quick to point out their strengths and very private in counseling on their weaknesses. Her biggest happiness came when she interacted with family; everyone knew she loved them unconditionally.

Friends

Dianne's friendships were incredible. She always became close friends with anyone she met. Her friends from high school and her college roommates continued to be in touch with Dianne until she passed away. Counting her friends is like counting stars; you will miss one if you try.

Dianne also befriended many strangers. It seemed she would take time to understand the needs everyone she met and their lives. She was always looking for ways to help.

Life of Service

Dear Jesus,

Sometimes I am afraid of letting you have complete control of my life. Show me how to be a "yes" kind of girl, like Mary was, and use me to bring you to others.

Amen

Dianne's passion was helping others. Dianne was an easy "yes" for any group that asked her for help and participated cheerfully. I would laugh and tell people that was her full-time job, but the pay was lousy. Dianne would always scold me in private because the pay was better than any other job on earth, so I quit poking fun. She would often remind me that her "earnings" are the best payment on earth.

Dianne was very private about her helping others. She did not like to talk about it because she did not like calling attention to herself. Dianne struggled during her cancer treatments to find the strength to continue helping others, but she never quit.

Dianne was involved in schools beyond the years our daughters attended. We were presidents of the Home and School Association, worked bingo on Sunday nights for years to raise money for the school, always volunteered to drive on school trips, organized parties, or did whatever was asked. Dianne was also very involved in the major fundraiser at the high school, volunteering hundreds of hours to raising money.

Dianne and I also were involved for four years with the God-teens program. Each Sunday during the school year we were blessed to have fourteen high school young adults come to our house. Our God-teens were wild and raucous freshman but quickly became family. Dianne had a very special bond with each of them. Dianne was quick on the compliment and always was genuine in her comments. Our God-teens gave Dianne so much love and happiness that she was sad when they started going off as young adults. She always said her reward was the events she could go to and support our "kids". She looked forward to their graduation and parties, their weddings, and their future lives. Dianne's faith was in action in her love with our God Teens and her commitment to their faith. Dianne's was in cancer treatment during the last three years of our God-teens experience, but she never wanted to miss a meeting. She was determined to show her love and support for our "kids" even though she was going through some of the toughest cancer treatments. This made her journey extraordinary. These young adults were quick to come and visit her, especially in the last month. The love and joy was incredible. You could feel the presence of Christ in these visits.

Dianne was continuously concerned with the challenges we face with hunger. Dianne loved volunteering at soup kitchens with her friends. She organized food drives, especially for the church pantry. I believe Dianne could have dedicated her life to helping the hungry. I believe her time working at soup kitchens were also some of her fondest memories. Dianne looked forward to talking with the people she was serving; in fact, she always talked about a man who called her "blue eyes" because he said her eyes were the most beautiful shade of blue on earth. She liked telling this story. One of her biggest challenges was helping the hungry and homeless. Rarely did she pass one on the street without offering some help. She even talked about the need to help the hungry during her last weeks on earth.

Long before her cancer, her passion for helping children in need grew stronger because of her involvement with Make-A-Wish Foundation. For nearly seven years she volunteered in the office every week and served on the board of directors. Dianne also worked as a wish granter, meeting with families and helping organize the wish. She would attend the funerals alone, often not telling us until afterwards, because she mourned the loss with the family. Dianne would decline any recognition for her work, insisting the recognition belonged to the family. She was just doing what Christ wanted. I believe her involvement helped prepare her for her own journey.

Dianne and I often talked about the struggles many cancer patients have getting chemo treatments. Dianne went to chemo practically every week during the last two years of her life. She and I would witness people in every stage of cancer, from just learning about it until hospice care. One of the great challenges we witnessed was the difficulty many cancer patients had in getting to the infusion center or hospital. Daily, it seemed like we would see someone pull up in a taxi or taxi-like service. What was really difficult were the patients that drove themselves to and from chemo treatment. Dianne knew how much of a drain on her body chemo was and to see these people struggling to get to treatment was tough. Some patients would even share about needing to go back to work that day because they could not afford to miss work. We struggled with how to help. Christ intervened by showing me a Facebook post for a fundraiser for the Heartland Cancer Foundation. This was just after Dianne had passed away and I was searching for a way to express our gratitude to the cancer center staff for all the love and care for Dianne. I learned how the foundation was created to assist with transportation expenses for patients in chemo treatment. I believe Dianne would get involved with this Foundation if she knew of it.

Dianne had a long list of charities, church, school and other causes that rewarded her with the opportunity to serve. God blessed her with a compassionate soul.

Enjoyment

Dianne enjoyed sports, especially football and baseball. I think she dreamed of being a football player or coach, but she would laugh about her lack of coordination. Dianne's passion was most apparent when she was constantly asked to solve a bet or dispute. I gave her a subscription to Sports Illustrated every Christmas, which was one of her favorite gifts. I was amazed by the number of twitter accounts of sporting individuals she was following. I remember often she was watching reruns of football games in the middle of the night while recovering from treatments.

Dianne was constantly reading. She has hundreds of books and usually read a book every week. Reading became a challenge for her, but she never quit. She enjoyed her soap operas, and in later years, several of the reality shows. I think she always dreamed of going around the world although she would never do the physical challenges or eat the stuff on The Amazing Race. She loved visiting with her friends, and later the nurses, about different shows. It was like a cult.

Dianne enjoyed to travel and visit new places. She especially liked long car trips so she could enjoy the beauty of America. She visited nearly every state and hoped to visit many countries. Her dream vacations included sporting events. Dianne also enjoyed going to Mass in new places whenever we traveled.

Dianne also loved animals, especially dogs. I hate dogs. Everyone knows it. I use to joke that our prenuptial did not allow dogs. Dianne did have a Buchan named Angel for several years. Angel was the bane of my life but provided Dianne great comfort until Angel became sick and died.

Life

A good analogy of Dianne's view on life is a glass of water. Consider you have a glass of water (or wine); now, take a sip. As you savor it, remind yourself of a good day in your life: maybe the day you accepted Christ as your savior. Maybe the day you met your spouse, or married, or the birth of your children. Take a sip for each of these good memories. Now remember a day when you were not at your best, when you were mad at your spouse or children, and take a sip for each of these days. This glass of water is analogous to how Dianne talked about life. Each day is a sip out of your glass of life. Now put it all back and do it again—ah, but you cannot. I often heard Dianne tell family and friends that you cannot ever regret or wish back any day. She believed that we cannot live life regretting the past. Forgive yourself just like Christ does. In the last few years she would also often say that every day is your "last time" for that day, so do not worry about or be sad about this being the last time you go somewhere, see someone, or do something because you can never reproduce the day. Dianne had dreams to visit many places, but she also did not regret not making these trips because she loved what she was doing every day.

Journey with Cancer

The Lord is my shepherd, I shall not want, he maketh me to lie down in green pastures, he leadeth me besides still waters, he restoreth my soul. He guideth me in the paths of righteousness for his name's sake (Psalms 23:1-3)

Dianne's journey with cancer began in April 2009. Her journey reminds me of the 23rd Psalm. On three occasions she faced a new stage of cancer and challenges. Psalm 23 reminds us of her cancer journey, from fear to eternal joy.

April 26, 2009

During Dianne's annual examination with her gynecologist she raised some concern about a "fat bubble" she wanted removed. Dianne wanted to have some minor outpatient procedure to remove a fat bubble from her breast. I was speaking at a banking conference in Las Vegas, so we decided to schedule the procedure for when I returned. I left for the conference.

April 27, 2009

Dianne went to a preparation for surgery appointment and a mammogram. I was backstage preparing to present the future of technology to 1,500 bankers and to lead a panel of bank presidents. Suddenly my phones started alerting me with emails and texts from both daughters and Dianne's sister. What is wrong with Dianne? Why is she in her bedroom with the door locked? I had no clue, so I called her.

The appointment was not what she expected. It included a biopsy. Dianne knew about the mammogram and didn't want to alarm me, I am not sure. But she was definitely not expecting a biopsy. During the biopsy the nurse commented "this doesn't look good." The doctor told Dianne not to worry and that he would have results back in a few days. Dianne was upset. Something didn't seem right. Dianne and I are good friends with the doctor, so I told her I would call him and find out more details. He told me the same thing; he really wasn't certain until he could review the test results. I called Dianne and suggested I immediately come home, which upset her more. This was the first of many dumb moves. I encouraged her to fly out to Las Vegas the next morning and relax until we knew the results. My conference would be over in two more days, so we would be able to spend some quiet time together away from all the questions and anxiety. She agreed.

It was time for my speech and panel discussion, so I went on stage but was in a daze trying to figure out what I was to do for Dianne. During the lunch break I made a room reservation at the Bellagio and booked her flight. The conference was at the Mirage so I could easily run between the resorts when Dianne arrived, and she would not have to see anyone. She could relax by the pool and not be bombarded with questions. Dianne liked the plans. She planned on resting, so I went to client meetings.

Dianne arrived the next morning at the Bellagio. My schedule was very light for the day, so I moved to the Bellagio to spend time with Dianne. We walked around the casino but really did not discuss anything important. Besides, we would not know test results until the next day. I wanted to skip the dinner and show at the conference but Dianne insisted I go, so I did. She planned on room service and sleeping. It was nice to have her there and to be together. But the anxiety was very high.

April 30, 2009

The next day the conference was wrapping up by lunch, giving me the afternoon to spend with Dianne. Dianne watched her soap operas and morning talk shows and was ready to go out for lunch. We spent the afternoon walking around the casino, waiting on the doctor's call. Voice messages, texts, and emails were piling up on Dianne's phone, but she didn't know what to say yet and didn't want to talk to anyone.

The doctor did call Dianne's phone but she didn't want to talk. She gave me the phone and asked me to call him. I found a quiet place to call him back. Dianne's doctor told me the news was not good and how sorry he was for Dianne. The biopsy showed abnormal cells, cancer cells. He explained several technical terms to me, but all I heard was cancer. I did not know how I was going to tell her. He helped organize a meeting the following week with an oncologist and surgeon to discuss options. He also ordered some medicine to help Dianne with the anxiety and sleeping. He shared his sympathy again, but I couldn't help thinking how difficult this call is also for him. I sat and prayed for a few minutes, but I knew Dianne was very anxious, so I found her and suggested we go back to our room. We walked quietly holding hands. I think she already knew the outcome but was hoping for a better answer. I still did not know what I was going to say.

I explained exactly what the doctor said. The cancer was likely just a small amount and she would have many options to consider. We sat there hugging and crying. We are never prepared for what to say, so I suggested we call our family priest. I called him, explained what we just learned, and handed the phone to Dianne. He embraced her with Christ's love with prayers and words of encouragement. I know it helped her. I went to get the medicine to help her rest. I do think we were in a good place for her to process everything that happened. She asked me to call our daughters. I also suggested I call her family and close friends whose texts she had not responded to for several days. She was not supportive of the idea, but I do think later she was grateful I did. She went to sleep so I started making calls.

It was a real challenge to make the first call to our daughters. I could tell they were very upset. I suggested they should not stay at work but go home. I struggled with every call, realizing there was no easy way to explain that Dianne had cancer. I was upbeat and optimistic, but I could tell both daughters were crying. I had to be alone to make each call because I could not hide my emotion. Both wanted to talk to Dianne. I suggested that they let her process the news for the day and call her tomorrow. I also knew that Dianne would be asleep with the anxiety medicine. I called Dianne's sister and explained why Dianne was so unresponsive. I then made the toughest call—to Dianne's dad. I could tell he was shocked. That was the call I finally used the phrase "breast cancer." I then called her friends. I thought my first few calls were tough, but these were harder. I tried to call their husbands first if possible so that I could practice what to say. There is no easy way to tell someone who loves Dianne that she has cancer. Dianne was always the one to serve others, not be served. Now she needed help but did not realize it and was not prepared.

Dianne was sleeping, so I went back to the conference hotel for dinner with clients. It was not easy to pretend nothing was wrong. Many questioned why I changed hotels; I am not sure how they knew. I kept looking at people wondering what would happen when I told them about Dianne. Dianne had a great community of friends in the people I worked with and our clients. So many people count on her for support and love; how will they respond? When the dinner was over, I asked a close friend to have a private conversation. I was going to tell someone in person. I was curious if I could without breaking downs. He was shocked. He wanted to help and was annoyed I was still participating in the conference; now he understood why I suddenly changed hotels. I asked him to keep this confidential because we were not ready to respond to questions, and there was more family to call first. As I walked back to the hotel, I was thinking of what I could do for Dianne for the next few days to help her prepare. Most every suggestion I made was quickly turned down because she just wanted time alone together—no shopping, no shows, nothing extravagant. Dianne and I relaxed by the pool and hung out in the casino, but mostly she slept. The anxiety and sleeping medication helped her fall asleep and not think about the future. Dianne started answering calls from our family and friends, which was good for them but not as good for Dianne. She still was having too much trouble processing the news and what it would mean to her. She refused to discuss it with anyone; in fact, I cautioned everyone not to bring it up. Even though she would have tougher news in the future, Dianne struggled to overcome the emotion of learning she had cancer.

May 4, 2009

Dianne's first appointment was with a surgeon. It was a strange appointment because he examined her, then rolled his chair back and said "I do many of these surgeries every week, but yours may require a senior surgeon. I made an appointment for you with our senior surgeon. Also, he needs more tests and more scans." No explanation. Just wait. We walked into the appointment believing she had a small lump that was a simple procedure and left without a clue as to what happened. Dianne was extremely stressed. We left the office and stopped by the church to see our family priest who blessed Dianne. Best move so far. Everyone was calling, wanting to know how the appointment was and what the plans were. We didn't know what to say. Dianne went into isolation again. Dianne was frustrated because nothing was being done to get rid of the cancer—just more tests and more doctors. I never understood why we met with this surgeon and not the senior surgeon. Why put her through this anguish? I was determined to be more aggressive with my questions from now on to prevent unnecessary pain.

May 6, 2009

After waiting two agonizing days, we met with the senior surgeon. He explained the location of the cancer was close to the breast-bone and had a thin margin. He explained her options of a lump removal, a mastectomy, or a double mastectomy. He explained if she wanted a mastectomy that he would remove all breast tissue, and a plastic surgeon would reconstruct at the same time. He explained the plastic surgeon would borrow muscle and tissue from her stomach to reconstruct. Dianne pulled up her sunglasses and looked at him quizzically saying, "So I am getting a boob job and tummy tuck at the same time?." We laughed. It was the first time in two weeks I saw Dianne's positive spirit. Although it would mean major surgery, she was going to rid herself of cancer in a few weeks and be back to normal soon.

The surgeon scheduled an MRI for a clearer picture. He also scheduled a genetic test so that we could evaluate the risk to her family. He also made us an appointment with the plastic surgeon and finalized a surgery date. She had a plan. Dianne needed a plan and action to give her something to focus on and a goal for being cancer free. This sounded like a plan.

Dianne was not interested in a second opinion. She trusted the doctors and wanted to get started and done: no more talking, just get it done.

May 7, 2009

The genetics test was a simple procedure. We learned a few weeks later that she did not have the DNA markers identified for breast cancer, so it was unlikely her cancer was genetic. Although not covered by insurance, this test gave Dianne peace of mind concerning our daughters, her sisters, and mother.

May 8, 2009

We met with the plastic surgeon. We explained what the surgeon said, and he laughed and told her that was not right. She could choose gel or saline. No tummy tuck. Although he looked her over and said she really didn't need it, he could perform it at a later time if she wanted. Dianne was upbeat and positive. She had a plan, and she really liked the plastic surgeon.

More tests. This time there was a very invasive MRI. We hoped we were done with tests but were determined to do everything to expedite the process.

May 13, 2009

Dianne met with the oncologist and learned more about her cancer. He explained her options for surgery but she was resolved to have a double mastectomy.

The oncologist also reviewed her likely treatment options— maybe some chemo and radiation based on surgery results. He also wanted more tests to make sure it was isolated to her breast tissues. He scheduled a PET scan and a CT scan. He provided us pamphlets and details on each of the procedures. I recorded several pages of notes planning to keep records for her. He organized several tests. We laughed on the drive home about all the medical jargon we were hearing without a clue of what it meant. It didn't matter; Dianne had a plan to get rid of the cancer and was focused.

I noticed we both were very diligent the first time to write everything down and try to learn what it meant. In later years, Dianne assigned everything a nickname, and we didn't try to learn it all.

May 15, 2009

PET scans and CT scans were long tests requiring no movement for hours. Dianne had to just lie still. She smiled on the way home saying she was done with tests and ready for surgery.

May 18, 2009

The day before surgery I was in a business meeting when my phone showed a call from the surgeon. I talked with him and he suggested I go home as soon as possible to be with Dianne. Unfortunately, the surgery was cancelled, and he recommended we go meet with an oncologist. Dianne was very upset. Not only was her plan no longer working, we were unsure what just happened. Apparently the tests showed something unexpected that needed an oncologist involved. This was another long night for Dianne.

Every change in plans resulted in a wave of phone calls to family and friends. The list of people I had to call kept growing; I made over twenty calls that night. I felt Christ's love with each call, but I couldn't help but be saddened every call. Dianne's friends came over, and the husbands joined me on the patio. It was extremely comforting to feel their love and presence with Dianne, even though she really was not up for company. It was the best thing for her and for me. We did not know what the future was going to be, but Dianne would say to trust in Christ.

May 19, 2009

Dianne was very nervous as we waited in the examination room. What happened, and what's next? We held hands in quiet. The oncologist was very direct. This was the second of difficult meetings in Dianne's journey. The complete results from the original biopsy included lymph node cells, and these cells also had cancer. The cancer was now identified in two areas of her body. In addition, the cancer was more widespread than first expected and was growing. The test results identified cancer in both breasts. A double mastectomy was her only option. He also believed she might have a few cancer cells elsewhere in her body but wasn't certain. The best option was to stop the spreading of the cancer before any surgery to prevent it from spreading elsewhere in her body. "Stirring it up with surgery was not the best option at this time," he informed us.

Her best option was aggressive chemo then surgery followed by radiation. He wanted to immediately start chemo, so she would need a "port" inserted into her body to use for chemo. This was an outpatient process at the hospital, and an appointment was made for Thursday. Chemo was set to begin on Friday. Chemo treatments will be every three weeks for at least six treatments. He would test her blood every week to monitor her blood counts and postpone chemo anytime the counts were too low. He would rescan her after three to four treatments to monitor progress and again after the sixth chemo treatment.

A "port" is a plastic tube that allows the chemo to be directly introduced into her bloodstream without having to find a vein in her arm every time. Typically, it would be placed on the upper shoulder near the heart. This required a morning in the hospital for the outpatient procedure.

Chemo is a short name for chemotherapy treatment. Each chemo drug is infused into her body by hooking up a drip bag to the port and letting it slowly mix into her bloodstream. Dianne's treatment would start with a bag of fluids that included Benadryl to relax her. Then usually there were three different chemo drugs in different bags of fluid. Finally, there was a flushing bag of fluids to clear any residuals from the port. The first and last fluid bag generally took about fifteen to twenty minutes. Each bag of chemo took about sixty to ninety minutes. These times would vary based on how much chemo was ordered. We understood there was a grand total that was divided up into each treatment and possibly could take an additional treatment to complete the grand total. Total time each trip averaged around five to six hours depending on the amount ordered and how busy the nurses were.

The oncologist explained more about the decisions Dianne would need to make and the impact they would have on her quality of life. This was a challenging battle, and he would monitor the effectiveness of the chemo and make changes to the drugs if necessary but would try to minimize the side effects. He explained how each treatment would compound the effect on her immune system to stop the cancer from spreading. Cancer takes advantage of the immune system, so the immune system had to be slowed. His analogy was a staircase. The first treatment was like going down a flight of stairs but only coming up a step short of the top. Each treatment would take her down to the bottom and back one less step until she basically could barely recover. Each time the side effects would be tougher to overcome. He said that she would need fluids on occasion and possibly blood transfusions if her counts were too low. If the test indicated the cancer was not as aggressive, then she would be ready for surgery followed by radiation to burn away any residual cancer cells. He would determine whether she was ready for surgery based on the scans.

He explained the side effects of chemo and answered questions on what to expect. Dianne would likely experience fatigue, nausea, loss of hair, loss of appetite, hand and feet numbness, loss of taste or confusion of taste, confusion or memory issues, and potentially osteoporosis.

Dianne was beyond distraught. Dianne's plan to get rid of cancer quickly became a major journey. We both were crying and hugging, not knowing what to say. When we left the meeting, we started driving. We drove aimlessly for thirty to forty-five minutes on dirt roads until we finally stopped. Neither of us wanted to face the questions at home. We stopped by the church and talked with our priest. He prayed with her and blessed her, which was the best medicine besides anxiety medicine so far. What started as a simple procedure—maybe a mastectomy within a month—was now chemo, major surgery, double mastectomy, and radiation, a six-to-nine-month procedure. There were no promises. Dianne needed time to be alone and process to pray and rest without sympathy and tears from others. Everyone knew this was going to be a challenging appointment, but this was worse than imagined. I prepared to call family and friends again with the news. Dianne's journey through the valley of darkness would be challenging and needed the prayers and support of everyone. Her faith gave her the strength to help her. She had a new plan but was scared. I also knew this would be another tough day for our family and friends. I was always amazed by how she was quick to comfort others but struggling internally with the challenge of cancer and the pending treatment. She would hug them and tell them that everything would be okay because her faith and Christ's love were protecting her.

May 20, 2009

The port surgery was smooth, although the hospital treatment was more like a procedure, not very personal. The doctors and nurses cared, but you were another bed and another patient on a checklist. I suppose this was part of how the individuals deal with so much pain and suffering every day. But Dianne needed to feel like everything was for her, to help her, to surround her with love and not be a patient on a checklist. We were on time but waited several hours because of scheduling issues. We learned to expect these challenges as normal every time we went to the hospital. Simple things like getting them to spell your name correctly or helping you when you need something to eat or drink were challenging. The good news was the hospital trips were rare. The cancer center was 180 degrees different. They greeted you by name, knew what you needed, and were prepared. Their first priority was Dianne. We loved the cancer center staff. We dreaded the hospital. Dianne received tremendous love and support at the cancer center, which embraced her like a person. The hospital was not as supportive. Although we went there many times over the seven years, she never had a good experience.

May 22, 2009

Dianne started chemo. Dianne was extremely nervous about the side effects but was happy that something was finally happening to get rid of the cancer. Her first day in chemo was very upbeat, and she immediately liked the nurses, who treated her like a queen. I was surprised how perky and upbeat she was after six hours of treatment. We went out to dinner with friends; there were no side effects so far. However, by Sunday she was extremely nauseated and could not get out of bed. She was very weak and had no appetite. In the meantime, with all the best of intentions, friends kept dropping off meals. Dianne would sometimes have enough strength to greet them with a hug and smile, saying not to worry. Unfortunately, even the smell of food made her sick. She was basically eating saltine crackers and drinking 7UP and water. That was all she could keep down. Each day she improved, and by the end of the week she was no longer nauseated but was generally weaker. The problem with nausea was she constantly threw up. And if she threw up, I threw up. I would run, a grab her a bag, and then stand behind her chair gagging while she threw up. She would scold me to leave the room, but by her side was where I was supposed to be.

Nausea was a major side effect. In addition, she struggled with taste. It was almost a daily test to see what tasted good today. Not only was taste impacted, smell was altered. I could not eat anything that smelled near her. I ate a lot of meals outside that summer. It was crazy because she was so warm and grateful with our friends that shared their love by bringing us food. As soon as they left, I had to find a place for it that did not make her sick.

Hair loss was the major side effect. First she noticed her hair thinning out. After two weeks it was falling out in clumps. She asked me to leave her alone one day, and she had the courage just shave it off. It was no longer easy to hide. The time had come for a wig. I suggested she make a party out of it, but she wanted privacy, no fuss. She wanted to continue to look as normal as long as possible. She never liked attention and did not want any unnecessary attention. I would always laugh with her when people would comment on her beautiful hair, and she was always gracious. What Dianne and I did not realize was that her hair would never grow back. She wore a wig the rest of her life as if it was her normal hair.

Chemo would continue all summer, occasionally postponed because her blood counts were too low. She continued to be weaker and required fluids to boost her energy. Going to the cancer center for fluids became almost a weekly process between chemo treatments because her blood counts were so low. On a few occasions she also need blood transfusions. Dianne didn't mind fluids, but she hated blood transfusions. She had to go to the hospital for blood transfusions. Fluids would boost her energy level and would take about an hour. Transfusions didn't seem to boost her energy level as much and would take nearly six hours. And every time we went to the hospital for a transfusion, it seemed like we had to start the entire paperwork process over.

That summer was an amazing rollercoaster. The side effects worsened with each chemo treatment. Each time would take longer to recover. We also became extremely cautious around germs because the chemo basically wiped out her immune system. We learned to plan events around her good days. We learned to preplan everything so she was protected and comfortable. But she wanted to continue a normal life. So we went to Vegas for a few days and enjoyed the sun and laughter. I became good at wiping everything she touched with sanitary wipes on everything from airline seats to pool chairs to everything in the hotel. Dianne would scold me for being too protective, but I was not going to change.

The first set of scans didn't show much progress, but the cancer did not look like it was spreading. While this was encouraging, her blood counts were low. We counted down the weeks until the end of chemo. The oncologist ran more tests and decided she was ready for surgery. Dianne was done with chemo.

October 12, 2009

Finally it was time for surgery. Everyone wanted to be at the surgery center, but Dianne did not want the fuss; she wanted privacy. I know this hurt many people's feelings but she was struggling with people helping her. Over time she would learn to let others help her by getting them involved. Surgery was at a private clinic with much better service than the hospital. We met with the surgeon and the plastic surgeon to review the procedure. The surgery would take several hours, and he would keep me up to date on progress. Dianne would need to recover in the clinic for a few days. I would also get a course in how to drain the fluid, change the dressings, and monitor her recovery. The plan was to start radiation after four weeks of recovery. Surgery went off without complications. I waited in her room where the surgeons visited with me, letting me know everything was going well. Dianne did sleep most of the next couple days, her spirits very upbeat. She believed she was about done with cancer. Life was going to return to normal soon.

Dianne was glad to be home, but I don't think she liked my nursing skills. We worked as a team to do what was needed. Dianne was trying to get use to her new body. I believe the surgery was more invasive than she imagined and understood. We didn't realize how much it changed and impacted her body. But she was glad it was over. We met every week with the oncologist to track progress until he believed she was ready for radiation.

We met the radiation doctor, who reviewed the radiation plan. It was critical to pinpoint the radiation precisely where the cancer was located so that he could burn up any residual cancer cells. He had to be careful not to radiate any vital organs or the new implants. He put two small markers on her chest to use for lining up the machine exactly the same for every treatment. The plan was to subject her to a total dosage of radiation in smaller doses until the total was satisfied. He would monitor how much she could tolerate and ease back on each dosage if the side effects were too much. Radiation was a daily treatment for thirty-eight to forty consecutive days with no break, seven days a week, even on Thanksgiving. This fit with Dianne's ambition to get it done. Dianne experienced similar side effects as chemo: the same nausea, loss of appetite, loss of taste, and so on. However, her determination to be rid of cancer focused her on pushing through the side effects.

A new side effect was the burns created by radiation. Radiation was always in the exact same location. After the first week it looked like a bad sunburn. The skin was mostly pink and red. The radiation area was from the upper shoulder area to below her breast and from mid-chest to under her arm. This area was all burned. In addition, she had some burn area on her back. After two weeks the skin was peeling away. By the third week the skin layers were blackening and disfiguring. All the work to have breast reconstruction was ruined by burning the skin permanently. Over time the skin would heal, but Dianne had radiation burns the rest of her life. What is amazing is how God created our bodies. The oncologist explained that surgery severed the nerves under her arm and in her breast area so Dianne never felt this side effect. Praise God. We rubbed ointments on the area several times a day to help restore her skin.

Dianne and the radiation doctor did not have a good relationship at first. I am not sure why, but she did not trust him. She did change and liked and trust him in later years but she was always uncomfortable. My guess is she reached a limit of how many people were poking and prodding her.

Week of Christmas, 2009

Radiation was done. The plan was complete. Nearly eight months since the initial biopsy had passed. The oncologist meeting was upbeat. Dianne would need to take some medicine and have some testing over the next five years. I was confused. I asked him if Dianne was cancer free, and he laughed saying the only way we would know that was an autopsy. I asked what tests she would need, and he said none. His explanation was that if they didn't get rid of the cancer then it was unlikely anyone could get rid of it. He told her there was nothing that could be done if there were even micro cells of cancer. He told me that he and I had better chance of getting rid of cancer because everything was done to Dianne and could not be repeated. Also, all the breast cells were removed. He told her to go live a happy life and not to worry.

Dianne was happy: she had a plan, and it worked. She was ready for the process to be over. It just seemed odd to me to do nothing but trust it worked. What started as a simple procedure, maybe a mastectomy was now chemo, major surgery, double mastectomy, and radiation. We celebrated by going on vacation to celebrate Christmas with the family. Dianne was ready to no longer be in the spotlight.

Cancer-free

Over the next few months Dianne gained back her strength and energy. She was back to normal. Her hair not growing back was a major concern which she constantly asked the doctors about but never received an explanation. I thought she was ready to punch one of the doctors because it was as if they didn't know or care. No one ever tried to help her. We would look for answers but never found any. We each have a few physical features that we take great pride in, and loss of these features is very devas- tating. Dianne's sources of pride were her skin and hair. Breasts are very important for all women. I witness Dianne's strength and self-confidence grow over time as she learned to accept her new body and disregard society's definition of beauty. Dianne also wanted to appear normal because she did not want to be the center of attention with people staring at her, wondering what was wrong. I know this was a daily challenge for Dianne because she never liked me or anyone seeing her body without the wig, and she constantly struggled to find clothes that hid the scars. Dianne was more beautiful to me every day, but I was challenged to make her believe.

Dianne believed she was done with cancer. We learned how hard it was to comfort someone not ready for comfort. Dianne needed to better understand what help she needed before help can be effective. Dianne was receiving offers for assistance long before she was ready. Dianne understood what help she needed only after she had a plan. This journey taught us many things, but most importantly we learned to trust and strengthen our faith. God provides us great comfort and guidance every day if we listen. Dianne used God's love to guide her from confusion to clarity, from fear to trust, and from comforting to being comforted. One of the greatest acts of love is to allow someone else, even a stranger, to help you. Dianne taught us how to see these acts of comfort as loving gifts from God. We witnessed "Thy rod and thy staff, they comfort me." We also learned that God does not love us for our outer beauty. We learned to take care of the body, the temple for our soul, but we will never know the real beauty of other people until we see their soul.

Dianne's Blessings

Cancer Again

Yea, though I walk through the valley of the shadow of death, I shall fear no evil; for though art with me. Thy rod and thy staff, they comfort me (Psalms 23:4)

April, 2013

Dianne started noticing a back pain that continued to worsen. She tried Advil but without success. She decided to go to urgent care one night but received no help. One night it hurt so bad I took her to the emergency room, and they ruled out kidney stones and other probabilities but did not find a cause. Over-the-counter medicine was the prescription typically. Another trip to urgent care didn't help except the doctor told her that he suspected something more serious and told her she needed to get it checked. Dianne would always dismiss it as a pain created by Pilates. She tried the pain medicine, but the pain was not going away.

May, 2013

Dianne had transitioned to a new oncologist during this time. Her original doctor moved to another practice. Dianne liked the new doctor and his staff, so she was agreeable to the change. During her next checkup with the oncologist, Dianne was insistent about the pain. He assured her the blood tests didn't show any reason for alarm. Dianne said, "You do not understand. I hurt; something is wrong." He suggested she have MRI and CT scans to see if there was anything that might be causing the pain. The tests were scheduled for the following day.

Whenever Dianne had tests and was waiting on results, she would hand me her phone. She wanted me to get the news for her. I would carry it around until the results were known. Usually we heard from the doctor's assistant within a day or two. These were challenging days because we feared bad news and prayed for an easy solution.

The next day I received the call that started another long tough day. The news was not good. The doctor wanted to see Dianne as soon as possible—that day, the sooner the better. She had cancer again.

We met with the oncologist who explained that Dianne had cancer tumors in practically every bone in her body. It was also clear her pain was the result of tumors wrapped in her spinal cord and growing in her hips. In addition, there were tumors in her liver. The cancer in her bones and liver were all from the breast cancer. The oncologist explained she had metastatic breast cancer, meaning the breast cancer was present in other organs of her body. She didn't have any breast tissue, but she had breast cancer again.

We went to the radiation lab and met with the doctor who explained the treatment. He tried to show us the scans, but all Dianne wanted was the plan to get rid of it. He was going to apply radiation to the spine and hips and continue investigating where else he should apply radiation. After the radiation that day, we went back to the chemo infusion center for the first of weekly chemo treatments. The oncologist also gave her a medicine cabinet of prescriptions including pain killers, anti-nausea, laxatives, appetite enhancing, anxiety and post-chemo drugs. He instructed her to take the pain medicine often to ease her pain. He explained that bone pain is the most painful experience anyone can have and to take as much as she needed.

While she was in treatment I started calling family and friends. These calls were as hard as the ones made about the original diagnosis because we thought she was done with cancer and now it was all over her body. Everyone was devastated. It was hard to comprehend why she had cancer again. Dianne was extremely upset because she thought she was done with cancer, but I think she suspected this was the pain after the urgent care doctor's comments, but she never shared that with anyone until now.

Radiation began that morning, attacking the biggest pain points and biggest tumors, several places in her hips and spine. There was no way to radiate all the tumors because there were too many. Radiation was daily for several weeks. Dianne would also receive radiation periodically over the next several months as tumors would grow.

Chemo was also started that day. The plan was to attack the tumors with radiation and slow the cancer spreading with chemo. Chemo was weekly with a week off every three weeks. Chemo would be at least five to six months, but new scans were planned for after the first three months.

This was an incredibly challenging day. Start the day with fear and uncertainty, learn your worst fears were true, be subjected to radiation and chemo, and now face side effects.

Dianne and I went to visit the priest after chemo. He prayed with her and gave her great comfort. Afterwards Dianne was incredibly upbeat considering she was facing cancer for the second time. She was very concerned that I didn't upset family and friends; she didn't want me to over explain what was happening. Dianne wanted to comfort everyone and was incredibly open to comforting her family and friends, but the radiation, chemo, and pain medication made her tire quickly. She wanted to talk with everyone, but she was too tired. And when she did talk, it would last very long. Amazing to me was her incredibly positive spirit and faith as she would say have hope and be positive because I will be okay. Christ is with me.

After four or five weeks of radiation, she no longer was taking pain killers because her pain was gone. She was considerably weaker but able to do most of her daily routine. I still did most of the grocery shopping, but she would go along to help. In fact, I became her driver taking her on her normal daily errands. I struggled to balance work with her needs, but nearly everyone I worked with were extremely supportive and helpful. Chemo was still a weekly routine and occasionally three or four days of radiation were needed. By fall, we even made it to a few of the Nebraska football games. Our new normal was planning trips around the treatments. She would get every third week off, so we leveraged these times for trips. We made a trip to Scottsdale to hang out with the family and a trip to Vegas with some friends.

August, 2013

After a month of radiation and three months of chemo, the scans showed promise. More radiation was needed and she had to maintain the chemo with scans again in three months. Dianne was mostly back to her daily routine but slowed on radiation and chemo days. Her stamina was dramatically reduced, making it very difficult to climb a flight of stairs. She also had to rest after any activity.

November, 2013

Dianne's health was improving. Her days were normal except the chemo days. She was back to her daily routine. Rarely could you tell she was sick. She was convinced she beaten cancer again. She was right! The scans were incredibly clean. A friend of ours who reviewed the scans told us he had never seen scans as bad as hers the first time that were so clean after six months. His believed Dianne's faith helped her beat the cancer again.

Dianne was normal again, and we celebrated with her. We would still make trips to the oncologist for weekly blood tests to monitor her progress.

Dianne and I rejoiced with gratitude to God for her cure. She fought the toughest pains and treatment challenges for a second time and beat cancer. Dianne would tell us that God helped her doctor and nurses make her well.

We celebrated with a long vacation for rest and relaxation. We prayed in gratitude for our blessing. We also resolved to treat every day as a gift and thank God every day.

Dianne was cancer free again. Praise God.

Dianne's Blessings

Cancer for Life

Our celebration was short lived. After three months, the oncologist decided he needed to run tests again. I am not sure what prompted the tests.

The oncologist's assistant called and wanted us to come to the office immediately. She was in tears and very upset. We were confused. The oncologist explained the tests results were not good news. Cancer tumors were everywhere again in her bones and liver.

The oncologist explained that Dianne would have cancer the rest of her life. Dianne needed to make decisions based on quality of life. Chemo and radiation would slow and maybe even cause it to go away, but the cancer would come back without treatment. He explained how there were alternative protocols or treatments she could try if this chemo stopped working. She would always need treatment to sustain life. This was the most difficult meeting of the entire journey.

Dianne was an optimist and believed she would be cured. She prayed for a cure and trusted in the doctors. In fact, she was determined to beat it again just like she did the other two times.

Dianne was so positive that we all believed. She was determined to endure any pain in order to be cured. I focused on making her remaining life long and full of love and peace. I was determined to protect her from unhappiness and fill her life with good memories.

Dianne started chemo and radiation immediately. The radiation would target the largest of the tumors and anywhere she felt pain. This radiation was every day and would last several weeks until the tumors were smaller. In addition, Dianne needed a new port, and to start chemo again we knew the procedures, so we knew what to expect.

When we went to the radiation lab and met with the doctor, he started to figure out that Dianne didn't need details, just action. All she wanted to know was when to be where and what to do. Quickly most of the doctors and nurses also understood her needs and didn't spend much time on details. I know they did what was legally required but Dianne was more interested in their lives and what she could do to comfort them, which was amazing.

This time our family priest full, of his Irish spirit, stopped by our house and prayed with her. This time Dianne asked him to hear her confession and provide her anointing of the sick. She was very different. In fact, she glowed with happiness after he left telling, me how she was free of all her sins. She was ready for the next step in her journey. She found Christ's comfort to help her prepare for the next step in her journey to heaven and wanted to share it with everyone.

Dianne was very different this time. Her struggle was how to embrace and comfort anyone who told her they were sorry or showed expressions of sadness. She was focused on sharing God's love. She wanted to reassure each one of them that she was going to be okay. She was receptive to having people come and see her although she was fairly drugged up from radiation, chemo, and pain killers. She was intent on comforting everyone and reassuring them she was going to be okay. Everyone came full of sorrow and left full of joy and Christ's love. Christ was at work in Dianne to help everyone around her, and she believed her mission was to do Christ's bidding.

The calls to family and friends were the toughest of her journey. Not only was she back in pain because had cancer again, she would always have cancer. Everyone was upset and reached out to Dianne for comfort.

Many people stopped by our house, which she welcomed and in fact kind of pushed for so that she could provide reassurance. The visits were usually brief because she couldn't stay awake very long because of the drugs. She was also struggling with side effects; she threw up virtually everything she ate. The side effects of chemo were back and compounded by issues from the pain killers. The pain killers were causing indigestion and constipation. I really struggled to feed her despite all the food generous people were bringing over. Nothing tasted good, including all fluids. She experienced mouth sores for the first time. Her energy level was low, but she could move around on her own, so her attitude was upbeat.

Daily communion for Dianne was the best medicine. Communion heals the soul of the celebrants, including her seven spiritual warriors who celebrated communion with Dianne every day heroes. Dianne's faith taught us to love our time together and trust in Christ. I know she was afraid of death, but this time she was very focused on sharing her faith with everyone and showing how you can be in difficult treatments and fighting cancer but have a life of joy and happiness. Many of our friends reflect on how she taught us to live.

The oncologist encouraged us to travel whenever we could, just to be careful with germs because her immune system was weak. We made several trips that spring. We developed a new rhythm for traveling by using a walker and sometimes a wheelchair. We planned our routes to avoid stairs. We were warned that her bones were very weak, and breaking a bone would be a disaster, so no heavy lifting was permitted. She accepted these changes so we could continue a normal life. We learned how to make it work and be normal about it.

A few stair steps were all she could handle and only if there was a rail for her to hang on. I bought her a walker to use around the house that we hid when company came over. The walker made it easier to move around without fear of falling, and she could sit on it when she had a task to do. I purchased a transport wheelchair to assist her getting around because she was weak and couldn't really walk very far without resting. I would push her to a destination and then she would get up and walk around. This was our new normal, and she accepted these changes in order to maintain her regular routine. I always loved watching her girlfriends grab her by the arm and help her do whatever they were doing.

To understand her weakness may be easier to understand if you consider how she showered. She could not stand very long, so we purchased a teak bench for her and a hand wand for washing. After she was done, she would have to lie down and rest before she could finish dressing and other things. I was amazed how independent she was and never complained because she needed help.

New scans were planned for May. Dianne was feeling weak and struggling with headaches on occasion but otherwise good.

Dianne was very optimistic and believed she was doing better and might be able to stop chemo. Unfortunately, the tests results were about the same. However, the oncologist decided to add an MRI to see if they could find a cause to the headaches.

Then, we received more bad news. Dianne's headaches were caused by cancer now in her spinal fluid and maybe the lining. The current chemo was slowing the spread of cancer in her bones and liver but was not preventing the cancer from spreading to other areas of her body. This change required a different chemo treatment for the bones and liver plus a new chemo that required injection into the spinal fluid. Additionally, some radiation on her head was needed.

The new treatment plan included:

- Chemo infusion through her chest port every week for two weeks than a week off. This was for her bones and liver.
- A new oral chemo of four pills twice a day for fourteen days. This chemo could potentially have major side effects.
- Radiation on the head in the areas where cancer was likely.
- Finally, the toughest treatment: Dianne would need chemo injected into her spinal fluid three times a week. The spinal injections were needed because the chemo cells were too big to get through the blood wall that protects our brain and spinal fluid. These injections involved out-patient treatment at the hospital. Each injection required pre-operation preparation, the operation (injection), and then six hours of lying perfectly flat. The operation generally would take fifteen to twenty minutes and involved removing existing fluid and then injecting the chemo. Dianne would tell me she didn't really feel anything once the needle was inserted. She would get a week off every three weeks. The oncologist would test the spinal fluid each injection to monitor progress.

The first few weeks went smoothly. Dianne didn't like the spinal injections because of how long we were in the hospital each time. The hospital didn't provide the rock star treatment she received at the cancer center, which did not help. Constantly she would be promised something to eat or drink but nothing ever showed up. She gave up after the first couple sessions and let me be her waiter. It was simpler. I do not think the hospital ever realized how badly she was treated. The weekly chemo injections for her bones and liver continued to go well, but the combination of both did slow her down and cause her blood counts to be often too low. But she was a trooper and hated to have any treatment delayed. It seemed every few days she needed fluids, and on a few occasions, blood.

She was doing so well we decided to take the family on vacation in Scottsdale during her week off. She was starting the oral chemo, and she didn't expect any issues. We could all relax and watch the grandkids swim. Dianne was unusually tired during the trip out. She also was not very hungry. She thought she had the flu that everyone else was struggling with, so the first couple of days she didn't leave our hotel room but dealt with flu symptoms. By the third day she was no longer keeping food down and was going to the bathroom constantly. She also thought she had a couple of canker sores. She was feeling miserable when everyone was having fun at the resort and she could not go anywhere. She tried to go to dinner one night, and it didn't last very long for her.

I decided to call her oncologist, probably a call I should have made three days earlier. What we didn't consider at first were the side effects. Dianne was warned about side effects, but I missed that discussion with the oncologist. Apparently the oral chemo will cause mouth sores, nausea, constipation, diarrhea, loss of taste, and swelling; blistering of the hands and feet; and difficulty sleeping. What we didn't consider was how the side effects were accumulative.

The oncologist was out of the country, so I talked with a nurse and she explained that Dianne didn't have the flu or canker sores; these were all the side effects. She also gave us a prescription for the mouth sores and the diarrhea. Dianne was so weak and dehydrated that she recommended we go to a hospital for fluids.

Dianne started the special mouthwash, and it made a big difference, but slowly. We also went to the closest hospital for fluids. The fluids really helped boost her energy, but the hospital was a long process because she was not a patient, so they required their own tests before administering any treatments.

Dianne was feeling much better, but we were worried about the flight home. It was important to get home because she had treatments the next day. What an amazing trooper she was on that flight, and we made it. I could tell it really wore down her body.

The next day the oncologist confirmed that she was dealing with side effects, so he cut the dose of her oral chemo in half. She was close to be over the side effects, so he started her on all treatments. She received chemo infusions for the bones and liver; she also went to the hospital for the chemo injection into her spine, and he started her on the oral chemo. His and our concern was the cancer would continue to spread without treatment. She needed everything to fight the cancer.

Dianne lasted almost a week on the oral chemo before she had to stop again. By now she was so weak she could barely stand and was requiring fluids every day. Her mouth was coated with sores and her hands ached and swelled, making it impossible to hold anything. We laughed at her "Fred Flintstone" feet that were covered in blisters, deep red and purple, and nearly three times normal size. Her ankles were often as big as her calves. Walking was incredibly painful. Her blood counts were so low that she required another hospital trip for blood transfusions. Dianne also struggled with the loss of taste and finding something good to eat or drink. Her biggest problem was mouth sores. At times the entire inside of her mouth plus under her tongue were coated with sores. Taste is not an issue when you struggle to put anything in your mouth or swallow.

Between the chemo injections at the clinic and at the hospital, and fluids, and blood transfusions, it seemed she was constantly in treatment. I would grab my work laptop and be with her while trying to keep up. This was our new normal.

Dianne was starting to experience new side effects from treatments. Dianne was also struggling with constipation and diarrhea caused by the pain killers. Dianne was encouraged to take them to deal with the bone pain, but she couldn't handle the side effects. She continuously had bladder infection. But these were treatable side effects.

The new challenges of neuropathy, focus, and memory were beginning.

This was an amazing summer because despite all the challenges, Dianne maintained a normal social and church life. Yes, the daily communion by her seven spiritual warriors helped. All the support from her friends to keep her involved also helped. Driving was no longer an option for her, nor was shopping. What was amazing during this summer was how Dianne never complained, never questioned why she had cancer. I noticed her attitude continued to transform in a very inspirational way. Dianne's faith and hope were infectious, and she would tell everyone that "I beat this twice and I will do it again." Dianne began to express her hope often and became very focused on caring for others both emotionally and in faith. One of her friends shared with me at the funeral that Dianne was comforting her and shared how she understood why some people "give in" to the battle and do not survive, but that she was confident she would endure and be better soon. Dianne was so positive in her hope and faith that everyone who came in contact with her would start with sorrow and sadness but leave feeling uplifted and happy. Dianne's faith and positive spirit brought happiness to many people during this treatment period, and soon everyone started to believe she would get better. I also believe the daily communion and regular visits from our family priest helped inspire Dianne to be angelic in her time with others.

I Am So Sorry

I received a call from the oncologist's assistant with bad news. She was crying. She wanted to make sure I was alone. We needed to come and meet with the oncologist right away. She kept saying how sorry she was for Dianne.

The oncologist explained the chemo injections in her spinal fluid were not working. He explained the cancer was still in her spinal fluid even after a few months of spinal injections. Continuing the spinal injections would not be effective. In addition, the oral chemo was probably harder on her body than cancer. There were many alternative "protocols" or options for the bones and liver when the chemo is no longer effective, but he needed time to find an alternative for the spinal fluid. We met again a few days later, and he suggested an alternative would involve implanting a port in her skull so the chemo could be injected into the spinal fluid reservoir in her brain. This is irreversible and extremely risky. However, it was not that uncommon for cancer patients like Dianne. Dianne was extremely weak at the time and barely able to walk, but she looked at him and said, "Let's do it." I was startled by her routine approach. This is a person who was beat up for an entire summer and now facing brain surgery who wanted to get on with it. I heard her explain to some friends that her only way to get better was to make this change. Amazing.

The assistant called me with instructions on meeting with the brain surgeon. She was still very upset because she loved Dianne so much. I didn't help matters when I asked how long Dianne had left to live. She checked with the oncologist and came back and said that likely three months if it didn't work and six months if it did. Dianne never wanted to talk about dying, so I didn't bring it up.

We met with the surgeon who explained the procedure with few days in the hospital following surgery. Dianne was very upbeat and did not want to create any anxiety for her family and friends. We talked with our family priest who reassured us that Christ was with us.

The surgery lasted a few hours and was very successful. In fact, Dianne received her first infusion of chemo through the port in her head the day after surgery. The new chemo injections were quick. Dianne could actually have the injections at the cancer center. At first I was very apprehensive to go in and watch, but after Dianne assured me it didn't hurt, I sat in the office while she received the injection.

Dianne found it easier to nickname everything, so these injections were called her "head shots." The process begins with some fluid being removed followed by another needle injecting the chemo. Usually Dianne would receive a bag of fluids following each procedure with some sedative and maybe anti-nausea medication. We were never sure, but it was a routine Dianne repeated two to three times a week for the next couple of months.

The oncologist would test the fluid withdrawn each time to see if cancer cells were present. After two months, no cancer cells were found, so the number of injections was reduced to once a week for a month, then every other week, and eventually once a month. Occasionally cancer cells or abnormal cells were found, so the number of injections was increased until it was clear several times in a row. Dianne's head shots continued for the rest of her life, usually with abnormal cells showing up every few months. I would always marvel how the women helping her during the treatment would chat with Dianne about reality shows and sports while the needles were going in and out of the port. I said to a friend one night that Dianne said she didn't feel a thing, but she told me in private it hurt, but she knew it would work, so she didn't mind.

Dianne continued this cycle of chemo in "head shots" and "body shots" for the next twelve months. As long as she was feeling good, there was really no need to change the treatments. Blood tests were run each week to make sure her counts were reasonable, but otherwise she was outperforming everyone's expectations.

We often talked about things she would want to do while she felt good. Dianne wasn't in a hurry to do anything extraordinary because she would often tell me she was doing what she wanted to do. I wanted to take her to Rome or London, but she preferred being at home visiting with family and friends, saving her energy to go to football games, baseball games, book club, out to eat, or family dinners. In Dianne's eyes, she had beaten cancer for the third time not by getting rid of it, but learning to live with the treatments and not letting it overcome her life. She often said it was like going to the dentist: it's just something you have to do.

Dianne was a voracious reader and loved to read. Much of her day was spent reading, but focusing for any length of time became a problem. She would also struggle watching a television show. She believed the pain killers were the issue, so she stopped taking them.

I also noticed that she would occasionally struggle with short-term memory. She was very good at quickly reacting to a situation and making up for it or laughing, calling it her "chemo brain." We would laugh at the oddest things she would say.

The memory issues and focus issues were beginning to be longer and more often. She also lost track of time, what day it was, and whether it was night or day. When she asked these questions on occasion people would remind her they had already answered the question but I told them to answer as if it was new question because of how frustrated she was when you reminded her that you already answered that question. I learned this slowly. One night she was napping, and I was napping on the couch nearby, and so I changed the channel. She perked up and told me to put it back because The Bachelor was going to be on. I tried to explain it was Friday and that show was not on, but she disagreed. So I put it back. Unbelievable. Later on one of the late night talk show the guest was the bachelor. Too bad she was asleep. But usually she was confused for brief periods of time.

A close friend visiting one day was asked to get rid of the bugs climbing all over the wall. The friend told me she got up and waved at the wall and Dianne was happy. Later they laughed about the "bugs."

By August, 2015 (a year after the brain surgery) the blood tests began to show the chemo was not as effective on her bones and liver. She also was starting to have liquid in her lungs. Scans really didn't show worsening, but did not show much improvement. The oncologist gave her a couple options to consider: a hormone treatment or another "harsher" chemo. Both had different side effects. He also suggested we consider interviewing hospice services. Dianne and I talked that evening about how it sounded like her options were becoming limited. We always knew there was no alternative to the head shots, but we hoped there were other chemo options available.

Dianne tried the hormone treatment first. This meant she only had to go to the clinic for blood tests and meetings with the oncologist, but not have chemo. She was feeling very good, and we made many of football games that fall. We even had a great trip to Vegas with many of our close friends. Our grandkids came to visit, so we had a special tailgate party celebrating Dianne and Holly and other friends' birthdays. What a great October.

Dianne was feeling so good that we planned to go to London over Thanksgiving. I booked the tickets and room, and we started planning our trip. Physically we knew the challenges, but her only concern was what if she needed fluids.

October 18, 2015

On Sunday, after everyone left, Dianne was watching the Packers, and I was working on my laptop on the patio, a fairly routine afternoon. Suddenly Annie came running out in a panic and said something was wrong with Dianne. I ran in and found her collapsed and having a seizure. I called 911. I tried to move her to the floor and keep objects away from her. I checked her mouth to make sure it was clean and found out how hard she could bite. The 911 operator worked with me until the paramedics arrived, and they started checking her. She started into another seizure, so they transported her to the hospital. I quickly followed, unsure of what to expect. I called a few family and friends to let them know what was going on and to have someone go hang out with Annie until the situation was resolved.

Dianne was completely confused and bewildered in the emergency room. It was clear she had no clue where she was or who I was. She kept trying to get up but we restrained her. The nurses were testing her and the doctor on call started examining her. He asked her what day it was, where she was, who she was, when was she born. She was confused. Finally, I asked her if the Packers won and she said sure and gave us the score. She was beginning to remember.

During the early part of the time in the emergency room, a priest stopped by to bless her. She was not sure what was going on, but when he started to pray with her, she did everything right! She said the right prayers and responses. Her Catholic education really kicked in.

A few hours after we arrived, she asked me what happened and why was she there. Dianne never remembered having a seizure. I explained what happened. Weeks later I overheard her laughing with some friends on how she got to ride in an ambulance with some cute paramedics and she doesn't remember it.

She stayed under supervision for several hours and was given anti-seizure medicine. Late that night the decision was made to send her home. She was happy, but I was in panic. What if it happened again? They gave me medication to give her and told me to call again. We were instructed to call the oncologist the next day.

Dianne went to sleep as soon as we arrived home. She needed rest, and so did I. I had a busy work day the next day plus going to the oncologist. But I didn't sleep much that night because I was scared she would have another seizure. In the past I would occasionally sleep on the couch next to her recliner but from that night on I slept on the couch every night unless she wanted to sleep in her bed.

The oncologist meeting was the toughest of the seven years. Just when you feel you have overcome the worst of it, the latest scans and tests showed the hormone treatment was not working and Dianne now had tumors in her brain. There was no treatment for the tumors. In addition, the cancer was at a point where treatments might be more harmful than the cancer. He wanted her to consider hospice. She did agree to meet with hospice companies and learn what services were available. She interviewed two groups and liked one particular nurse very much. So we were prepared for hospice although she didn't think it was necessary. She wanted to continue chemo. The oncologist said we would try another protocol, but it was going to be harsh.

The new chemo would require her to have her hands and feet wrapped in ice packs to slow the impact of blistering. Dianne was very tired but upbeat and insisted on her normal daily activities. The next day was a surprise party for Dianne's close friend, and Dianne insisted on being there. A few days later one of her book club's Christmas party was a dinner party that she enjoyed celebrating with her friends. I laugh because on the first trip I barely could lift her into our car, so on the second trip she insisted that one of our friends drive her because his car was easier to get into. He and I knew better than to disagree.

We celebrated Thanksgiving at her parents' house and started the treatment. This chemo would be a once-a-month treatment, if it worked. She would also continue the head shots. Her oncologist said it would use up the remainder of her bone marrow, but why not give it a try?

Her friends organized a big decoration party. Several came over and decorated our house with Dianne sharing with them where things belonged and Annie's leadership filled in the gaps. Dianne has so many beautiful Christmas decorations especially her collections of nativity scenes. Everyone was full of laughter with my job keeping the wine available. I know Dianne enjoyed decorating, so this was a good substitute for her enjoyment.

Pray for Dianne and thank God for her family and friends.

Peaceful Journey to Heaven

Thou preparest a table before me in the presence of mine enemies. Thou hast anointed my head with oil; My cup runneth over. Surely goodness and loving kindness will follow me all the days of my life; and I shall dwell in the house of the Lord forever. (Psalms 23:5-6)

Dianne began her journey to heaven in December 2015. Her last days mirrored her life, full of faith, charity, joy, and happiness. Dianne was full of laugher and optimism. Her body was dying, but her soul was alive and full of Christ's love. She never complained or talked about dying. Our home was full of family and friends highlighting every moment.

December 12, 2015

I finally convinced her to let me buy a lift chair for her so I could move her better. She did not want me to spend any more money on her. She told everyone not to buy her anything; "Save your money," she insisted. It was her way of saying she was at peace with our presence and didn't need anything else. Thank you, God.

Dianne was running a very high fever. I called the cancer center to ask what to do, and their recommendation was to take her to the hospital. The concern was the fever could be a sign of a potential seizure or worse. We arrived at the hospital and talked with the nurses and doctors who wanted to run some tests. After we sat around for several hours, the hospital decided to keep her overnight. I texted her oncologist who recommended I take her home, but the hospital wanted to keep her. Dianne was taken to the cancer level and checked in around midnight. I sat with her until about 2:30 a.m. while the hospital was filling out paperwork and introducing everyone to her. Dianne was going to sleep, so I went home to sleep.

December 13, 2015

When I got back to the hospital at 8 a.m., she was extremely upset with me because I left her. She was confused. She didn't understand where she was and why she was there. She was hungry and thirsty, and no one would bring her anything to drink or eat. She was constantly disturbed to take her temperature or introduce a shift change, but no one brought her anything or any pain medicine. They explained how busy they were and that they would bring her something after helping the other patients on the floor. I promised her I would not leave her again. I watched her ask for pain medicine and water and then wait a long time for a response. I went and found it for her. It was obvious her confusion was real.

I talked with her oncologist that morning, and he recommended Dianne start hospice. I talked with Dianne, and she did not want to stop chemo. I called our priest, who met with us that afternoon and discussed this option. Dianne didn't want to stop chemo because she felt like she was quitting. The priest earned his stripes in how he explained to her that hospice was the best treatment for her. Later that evening Dianne and I discussed that starting hospice did not really mean stopping chemo because her next chemo treatment was not until end of month, so hospice could help her rebound enough to be strong enough for chemo.

Early in the day Dianne asked me to get her something. She knew what she wanted but couldn't explain it very well. I tried to guess what it was, and she became agitated that I couldn't figure it out. She told me Annie would know what it was, so I called Karen and Annie, and she talked to them, but they were equally confused. I called one of her friends and explained the challenge, and she had an idea. She showed up that evening with a soft cuddly dog, and Dianne was so excited. Someone had figured it out. What a blessing. She found great comfort in holding the dog, we think, because it reminded her of her dog from a few years earlier. God bless her friend for giving Dianne relief in the hours of need.

I slept in a chair and kept an eye on her all night.

December 14, 2015

The next morning, the hospital doctors, nurses, and Dianne's oncologist met with her and explained her options. Our understanding was that the only way to leave the hospital was to agree to start hospice that day. They explained her lungs were full of fluids and she had blood clots that could cause a heart attack or worse. Her option was to sign the Do Not Resuscitate paperwork and start hospice. I witnessed the greatest act of courage when Dianne signed the paperwork. She wanted out of the hospital. We agreed to meet the hospice staff at our house and left the hospital.

A friend of Dianne's stopped by to comfort Dianne. Dianne was very tearful because of the challenges she learned from the doctors. A simple hug and reassurance of God's love was timely from her friend as we left the hospital.

Dianne was just glad to be home and return to her routine. Her treatments were over, but we were unsure what hospice treatment meant. Dianne was struggling with the change because she found comfort in the cancer center staff every week and would no longer see them. She was concerned by the sorrow she created for the staff and she would not be there to tell them she would be okay.

The hospice team met with us and explained the change in treatment. Hospice was a change in treatment. No longer did she take any of her old medication. New prescriptions of pain killer and anxiety medication were delivered, and the nurse showed me how to administer the drugs. No more pills; instead, everything would be liquid. From now on we focused on keeping her out of pain and comfortable. The same nurse would come and examine her every day as well as assistants who would show up and help her bathe and dress. Another assistant would come and massage her. That was the plan: the same people, every day, at the same time. Dianne liked her nurse and so accepted the change quickly. The communion that day was especially powerful medicine for her spirit. I witnessed her become more angelic that day, and for the remainder of her life her spirits were very high. She was glowing with Christ's love, and everyone witnessed it. God bless our heroes.

December 15, 2015

Rosary and prayers were shared continuously with Dianne. Her close friends came by every day often just to pray. Every Tuesday her friends would gather and kneel around her chair and hold her hand and pray a rosary and other blessings. Afterwards Dianne would tell me she would sleep during part of the prayers but her friends always said she said Amen at the right times. God's presence was real. I often hid in my home office because my grief was overwhelming. Our bedtime ritual was often me holding her hand and praying a rosary as she slept. Our house was always full of God's love especially during the last month when hundreds of friends came by to pray with Dianne.

December 16, 2015

Unfortunately, the hospice process was not as smooth as we believed. Different nurses would show up, and we would have to go through the introduction process repeatedly. Dianne was confused. I warned people never to be in hospice during holidays because the offices are closed and only they came out in an emergency. We convinced Dianne this was okay, but I really struggled with the lack of support from the hospice staff. We debated having Dianne check into a hospice center, but she really did not want to leave home, and neither did we. But I was concerned that I would be alone without support if something happened.

The hospice team stopped by one afternoon and wanted to help us with funeral planning. As polite and quickly as I could, I ask them to leave. This was the first and only time that Dianne and I were involved in this kind of discussion. The time had already past for a good time for this discussion. We were focused on enjoying living and not thinking about dying. Dianne knew she would always have cancer, but on so many occasions over the last two years she "beat" the odds and rebounded, and so she considered this another setback she would overcome. However, her body was definitely struggling.

December 17, 2015

I often asked if she wanted to go visit the nurses at the cancer center, but she would say they were busy and didn't need visitors. She had mixed emotions, so I quit asking.

Dianne continued to be very upbeat, but her ability to stand and walk was deteriorating quickly. She also started having longer periods of confusion. She also could not focus easily even in conversation. She would laugh about it and so would we. She also lost concept of time. Often she would wake up in the middle of the night wanting breakfast. So I made it. There was no reason to argue or try to explain; our goal was to keep her encouraged and comfortable.

Slowly she lost the ability to stand. At first I could stand her up and she could use the walker to get around. Later she would ride on the walker as I pushed her around. Our routine was for her to put her arms around me and I would lift her up. We laughed that night when I was lifting her because I asked if she was trying to make a pass at me and she laughed and said I would know it if she was. Eventually Dianne no longer had the strength to stand up. Yet she never complained; she accepted the changes and laughed.

I would find her clothes each day and help her dress. So often I would bring her a top that didn't match the pants, so she could scold me. I knew she was beginning to lose focus when she no longer complained. I couldn't let this upset me because everyone else needed my support. I also would not let myself consider the future. These moments were too precious as Dianne shared her love.

She often asked if it was Christmas yet and when were we going to open presents. Where was everyone? She now needed pain killers and anxiety medicine every few hours. It was apparent she was fighting to make it to Christmas, but she never gave up hope.

Hospice would increase her dosage slowly every few days. Her body was starting to shut down. The nurse shared with me it was a matter of weeks at best.

December 18, 2015

Julie and her family were planning to come to Lincoln for Christmas. We were very excited to have everyone together celebrating Christ's birth. Julie and I often talked about her family coming from Phoenix to Lincoln earlier than planned. Julie was anxious to be with us helping Dianne.

Later that night our home became full of laughter when Julie, Chuck, Holly, and Trey arrived. Dianne was very upbeat and kept us on our toes. Christmas was Dianne's favorite time of the year. It was fun to have both daughters and our grandchildren running around and everyone home. Dianne was still in charge. Dianne would often tell us to feed the kids because they were "hangry" (angry because they were hungry).

We discussed moving Christmas celebration up a week because of Dianne's health, but Dianne didn't want to change the plans.

Julie and Annie had a fire drill planned in case Dianne had a medical emergency. The plan was for Chuck to load up the kids and leave until the "all clear." We all knew Dianne could have a heart attack or worse at any time and that no one would be available to help. I am not sure what my actions would be so I prayed constantly for a miracle. We knew from the hospice staff that Dianne's body was beginning to fail, so we all continued to comfort her.

December 19, 2015

A surprise visit by our God-teens provided great joy. She visited with each of them and loved having them hang around for a while. I could see she was struggling to stay awake, but she was not going to miss this chance to share time with the God-teens. God bless these incredible young adults for making Dianne's life so full of love.

December 20, 2015

Our home was constantly visited by family and friends. Dianne was always upbeat and full of laughter, often making fun of her "chemo brain." She never complained, but it was obvious the pain was getting worse. She enjoyed the visits of everyone during this time.

No longer did anyone need to call. Her close friends came to be with her constantly. What an amazing act of love and courage. We are grateful for celebrating Christ's birth with Dianne and the special courage and love of her friends.

Dianne memory issues continued to worsen, but she would often say something and then laugh. We were preparing dinner and someone asked what temperature to cook the meat and Dianne yelled out 238, and then paused and starting laughing, saying she had no idea where that came from. So many stories of confusion led to laughter.

Dianne no longer worried about her head—her wig. She did keep a ball cap handy but only on occasion did she wear it. Her beautiful eyes and smile would quickly melt away any sorrow. Her wit would always get a laugh and put everyone at ease.

Dianne maintained her positive spirit and need to comfort others. Everyday more people stopped by to see Dianne. I think everyone wanted to share her love one more time. She had hundreds of visitors this month. Many were people we had not seen in years. Her sister's family was around every day to help her feel normal. Dianne was able to reassure each person that Christ was with her and she was going to be okay. She made sure she always hugged or held hands with everyone who came and made sure they understood she was going to be okay and they should be at peace and pray. What an amazing soul to think only of others.

December 21, 2015

Our family priest organized Mass at our home again. Our home was full of thirty to forty family and friends celebrating with Dianne. The Holy Spirit moved all of us to be thankful for God's love and the Eucharist. The priest also anointed Dianne reflecting on the prior Mass with the God-teens when he anointed her. Everyone witnessed God's love present around Dianne. The priest often reflected on how his faith was strengthened by witnessing the God-teens at the previous Mass and all the family and friends attending this Mass.

Dianne was angelic in her care for everyone who came and made sure to comfort everyone who came to visit. So often her friends would kneel and ask Dianne to pray for them. She would hold their hand in love and tell them she was going to be ok. Amazing.

December 23, 2015

That evening we were napping when the doorbell rang. We were not expecting anyone, Dianne was a sleep in her chair, and I was napping on the couch. When I opened the door I was surprised to see twenty or thirty young adults who wanted to sing Christmas carols for Dianne. What a beautiful act of love. Dianne loved the music and although she couldn't really see them, she was very attentive. After a few songs, one young man asked her what was her favorite Christmas Carol. She said it was "Silent Night." They had just finished singing "Silent Night," so were a little confused. I asked her again and she insisted it was "Silent Night." She wanted to thank them again for sharing their time with her. I quickly tried to think of another song and the only song I could come up with was "Little Drummer Boy." Again their singing was so beautiful we both were inspired by their presence. God bless these young adults for taking time to give Dianne so much joy.

December 24, 2015

The hospice nurse believed it was a matter of days and maximized her dosage of pain killer and anxiety medicine. I was very uncomfortable giving her the medication because I felt like I was drugging her too much. The challenge was she never really said it hurt anywhere. Her legs were restless and we would rub them, but it didn't make a difference. When I tried to stand her up, she thought her leg was broken. It may have been. The hospice team said to increase the number of doses of pain killer.

We received a call from one of Dianne's spiritual warriors who wanted to bring a relic by and bless Dianne. The relic included actual wood from the Cross of Christ. Our family gathered around her as he shared the prayers of the relic. He then helped her hold the cross and kiss and pray while holding the cross. Each of us held the cross and prayed for Christ's love for Dianne.

We all gathered around Dianne and opened presents. Our Christmas Eve tradition was Mass followed by dinner and opening presents. Karen, Scott, Tyler, and Morgan always joined in the festivities, everyone trying to guess the gag gifts from the real ones. Dianne did not want any presents, so all the gifts were for the young ones with a few gag gifts.

Christmas, 2015

Christmas day was special. Dianne's family came for the celebration. Dianne was tired but full of happiness celebrating with everyone. What a great day. No one wanted it to end. Dianne slept through opening presents and seemed bummed about missing it. Her parents and siblings spent the entire time gathered around Dianne laughing and telling stories even though Dianne was asleep most of the time. I always tear up thinking about her parents saying goodbye that day. They raised a beautiful daughter who was now preparing for heaven. God comforts them every day, and so does Dianne.

December 27, 2015

We needed to make a few decisions on whether Julie's family should stay or return to Phoenix. We decided to celebrate Julie's birthday and then have them go home. We didn't know whether Dianne would be with us for days, weeks, or months. We had a happy night full of laughter to the point Dianne scolded us for being too loud. Dianne had salmon and lemon pie for dinner, by chance two of her very favorites. This turned out to be the last time she was able to eat.

December 28, 2015

Julie, Holly, Trey, and Chuck spent some time alone with Dianne, kissed her goodbye, and left for Omaha to fly home. Annie went with them to help, so Dianne and I were alone, and we cried, holding hands. We felt so much love and joy from Christmas. We didn't ever say a word, but we knew it was their last visit with Dianne.

I decided that evening that a few of her friends would like to visit her if possible. I could also sense she was starting to slowly lose her ability to speak. I called and invited a few to come over, and soon we had a houseful of people praying the rosary several times. The family priest joined us. Dianne insisted I get them something to drink, and soon it turned into a wake with Dianne. She slept even through the laughter but was quick to hug goodbye each person. Late that night I sat with her and prayed the rosary. I would give her medication every four hours, but she was not responding much.

December 29, 2015

Dianne could no longer swallow, so we swabbed her mouth with water. Dianne was much less responsive, only responding to direct questions or comments. Her murmuring became difficult to understand. We knew she was cognizant because she answered questions and responded directly to people. Her friends came to pray the rosary with her again. This time more people came. Over thirty people kneeling and praying around Dianne. The Holy Spirit was very evident to everyone. A friend shared with me she whispered to Dianne her love and Dianne squeezed her hand. She knew that Dianne was telling her she would be ok. After a few hours I noticed many were still there, so I grabbed a couple bottles of wine and starting filling glasses. Several bottles and hours later their husbands showed up with food, and we had another lively wake underway. This wake lasted until late that night and included another visit from our family priest.

December 30, 2015

On Wednesday, the rosary group showed up early in the afternoon and spent most of the day with Dianne. Later that evening more friends came by, and we celebrated around Dianne again. She would love the parties she was hosting and the joy we shared. Dianne was no longer responsive and labored in her breathing. Our priest again blessed her many times. I could sense no one wanted to leave. We all realized that her time on earth was slipping by, and everyone wanted to be there with her. After everyone left, I prayed with her again for a while, gave her pain medicine, and dozed on the couch.

Dianne showed us how Christ will lift us up with grace and compassion: never complaining, always reminding us of the joy and peace. These last few days were very spiritual, providing everyone who came here a powerful sense of Christ's love. The focus was not on her dying; it was on the celebration of life. Everyone wanted more. Dianne showed all of us how to confront our death with grace and dignity.

December 31, 2015

About three thirty in the morning I woke to check on her. I am certain it was Dianne telling me it was time for her to go to heaven. She was breathing faintly. Christ helped her peacefully complete her journey on earth. I held her hand for a while, praying for her soul. I knew my soul would always be with her. My love will always be Dianne. I always depended on her to help me in times of need. I needed her at this moment. I started missing her that moment and continue to miss her today.

I knew I needed to help our family and our friends. Each day everyone was preparing for this moment, but we were still at a loss. I woke up Annie and let her know that Dianne passed away. I called Julie. I reminded both of them that Dianne loves them and so did I. I called Dianne's sister and let her know Dianne passed away. I then called the hospice nurse. She called the sheriff and came over to our house. I realized my close friend was at church for his adoration hour, so I called him. He and his wife came over. I called a couple other friends, and they also came over.

The hospice nurse was a rock star. She was very patient. The two sheriffs were also very good as they helped me through the process. When it came time to examine Dianne, I asked our friends to wait in my home office. Annie, taking after her mom, was busy getting everyone coffee. The sheriff then asked me to bring out all of Dianne's medication for review. I was shocked when it completely covered our kitchen counters. The nurse destroyed all medications as required, and the officers kindly comforted me and left. I invited everyone back into the living room. The hospice nurse said we could call and have family or friends come over before we called the funeral home. We had so much love with our family and friends that I felt it was time. The men from the funeral home came, and when it was time to move Dianne, I asked everyone to wait in the office again. By now Dianne's sister, our friends, and Annie were present. What a beautiful time.

While the funeral men were moving Dianne, it occurred to me that I should retrieve her wedding rings. She named one Julie and the other was Annie. She also had another ring she always wore that she named Holly. These were the only things she ever talked about giving someone when she passed away.

I was holding the rings and walking to the back of the house feeling tremendous grief, not knowing what to do. I walked into the office and asked what I should do with her rings. Annie was incredible. She jumped up and grabbed them saying, "I will wear the Annie ring, Karen you wear the Julie ring until she gets here." She asked another friend to wear the Holly ring until she gets here. Wow, that was easy.

By the time I went back to the living room, the men had Dianne ready to take to the funeral home. I walked out and watched them put her in the van and watched as it pulled away. I was lost. I did not know what to do.

Most everyone decided to go home and rest for a while. In a few hours we would need to meet at the funeral home to plan the funeral, and everyone agreed to help me.

A few friends stayed while Annie went to rest. I tried but suddenly the grief overwhelmed me, and I sobbed for a long time. I contacted the rest of the family and shared the news of our loss. I also emailed numerous people who were always visiting or in contact with Dianne. I was sure my friends were also sharing the news. Although we knew for several years and could prepare for our loss, the experience was still difficult for everyone.

In preparation for the funeral home meeting, I was asked by the funeral director to bring some clothes to the funeral home for Dianne. I stood in her closet, stumped for some time, debating what to do. I finally narrowed it down to two outfits and let her girlfriends vote on it. We also agreed that Dianne would like to have her Tiffany "d" necklace. When I looked in her dresser I was surprised by how many drawers were full of blue "Tiffany" boxes I found. All I could see was thirty-seven years of getting out of the dog house, anniversaries, Christmas, birthdays, and other special occasions. I began to ponder what was I going to do with all this stuff.

Annie, Karen (Dianne's sister), Morgan (Dianne's niece), and several friends met me at the funeral home. I suggest if you are faced with the challenge of planning a funeral to take a group of people to help. We had to write the obituary listing: family members names, dates, and so on. Dianne was always the source of this information, but as a group we collected it.

Christian music is very special to our family, Dianne and I had many favorites. I teared up when it was time to choose the music. However, I called a close friend and asked her if she would sing for Dianne's funeral, and she told me she was praying all morning that I would call. The only condition I had was she had to choose the music.

It was time to pick out the casket. The room was like a car sales room: different colors, makes, and models. The group spread out commented on what color, style, and lining Dianne would love— the brown with black; no the black with brown. Finally, the group narrowed the choice to one. A friend was standing with me in the corner whispering to buy the cheapest, but I knew this group found comfort in the shopping. We repeated the process for the grave box.

The next step was the cemetery. A close friend suggested Calvary Cemetery, so he took me there. Dianne and I did not talk about funeral arrangements, so I was praying I was doing what she would want. We agreed a few years ago to be buried in Lincoln during the time we prepared our wills. So I knew I was doing the right thing. However, the cemetery was closed for New Year's Eve. My friend showed me around and where his family was buried. I felt a great peace there, but I was struggling with the thought of Dianne in the ground. He showed me the mausoleum, which was especially beautiful because Mass is held in the mausoleum every week. Dianne so loved Mass; I believed this was a peaceful and beautiful place for her. We finalized the planning and prepared for family to arrive.

My brother came that day and helped tremendously with the preparations by making several trips to restock our beverages. Over the next several days our home was full of family and friends, so we had to restock a few times. Food was continuously showing up, which are incredible acts of love.

Sunday, January 3 was the day of the rosary. I struggled to sleep the night before. I woke early and went to Mass early because I needed to be at the funeral home mid-morning to check on Dianne. I could not help but cry through the Mass. I remembered how much Dianne loved Mass and sobbed. I couldn't believe my luck: the children's choir sang two beautiful songs—"Silent Night" and "Little Drummer Boy." I sobbed. What are the odds that they would choose the two songs from Christmas caroling?

As I left Mass, our family priest stopped me, asking, "What are you doing at 8:30 a.m. Mass? I wrote my homily on Dianne for the 11 a.m. Mass. The homily today is on the Three Wise Men, and I am using Dianne's life as well as another longtime parishioner and a priest that also passed away recently. Incredible. Driving to the funeral home, I wept thinking about the day. I was also on my way to check her makeup. This was the first time I would see her since she left our home a few days earlier.

No one was around when I arrived at the funeral home. I looked into the chapel and saw Dianne. I kneeled next to the casket and held her hand praying Our Father. When I saw her face I was overcome with the greatest joy I had felt in several years. Dianne was so beautiful, and I felt her presence directing me to be at peace. I couldn't cry anymore. In fact, I was full of Christ's love through Dianne the remainder of the day.

Dianne's sister Karen was an incredible help throughout all of Dianne's journey but especially during these last weeks. She joined me at the funeral home, and we finalized Dianne's appearance. Dianne always had sunglasses on her head so I knew I needed to bring them and put them on her.

I went back to Mass and join some friends. What a beautiful Mass and incredible homily. Our priest talked about the gifts we each can share. I was full of joy.

I went back to the funeral home and spent the afternoon during visitations meeting family and friends, trying to provide comfort and sharing Dianne's love with everyone. An amazing number of family and friends came and talked about Dianne. So much love.

We met at the church that evening for the rosary. I was amazed by the hundreds of people who came to celebrate Dianne's life. Afterwards over a hundred stopped by the house for support. Dianne loved a good party, and this wake was one of the best. What started as a difficult day became a day of joy and celebration for Dianne.

Dianne's celebration of life was on January 4, 2016 at Saint Joseph Catholic Church. The church was packed with Dianne's friends and family. I was amazed by the outpouring of love. The singing was so beautiful I cried, not because of grief, but incredible joy I felt from the beauty of the music and the family and friends gathered for Dianne and Dianne's beauty. I knew she would approve.

Dianne's seven spiritual warriors that brought her daily communion also participated in her funeral. Her friends helped with readings and singing, each talking about the honor they felt for helping Dianne. Each will tell you they benefited more from helping Dianne and strengthened their faith. Each of these friends and our family priest were all God's instruments for us. I pray for these people knowing each will join Dianne in heaven someday.

I was grateful to God for how beautiful were Dianne's last days on earth. Our house was full of faith, family and friends, reflecting Dianne's life. Daily prayer and rosary sessions intermingled with wake-like celebrations. Laughter and love melting away the sorrow. Hundreds of people stopping by to pray with Dianne one more time. These days could not be planned but could not be more perfect. Amazing.

Dianne's journey on earth was complete. She served her Savior with acts of compassion and charity for others. She also served her Savior with a loving spirit and unwavering faith. Christ gave her a life a joy and happiness, love from everyone who knew her. Dianne's final gift for me and everyone was her peaceful journey to heaven. I worried so often about another seizure, a stroke, or worse. Dianne gently completed her life on earth as a final act of compassion for everyone. God bless her soul.

Journey with Faith

O Lord of hosts, hear our prayer, Harken, O God of Jacob! O God behold our shield, and look upon the face of your anointed. (Psalms 84:8-9)

Our family priest would comfort us throughout the journey. Dianne loved him, especially his stories about growing up in Ireland. We were honored to visit his native country with him and several friends and always found comfort in his prayers. His blessings helped Dianne strengthen her faith. He reminds me the mysteries of God's grace are working in ways we cannot imagine. Consider the mysteries we experienced.

We meet many souls during our time on earth that make our lives better. Dianne's was an ordinary Catholic who lived an extraordinary life. During the first two rounds of cancer, Dianne struggled with her fear of the darkness and the future. However, Dianne's transformation happened when she learned she would have cancer the rest of her life. Suddenly she no longer worried about herself; she became devoted to comforting and serving others. God blessed her with the gifts of charity and compassion. Her focus was blessing by sharing Christ's love. Even as her body began to fail, she still found a way to share Christ's joy and happiness. She lived full of charity and compassion. She showed us how to pass away without grief. Dianne did not want to die; in fact she believed in a miracle. Dianne's miracle did happen, but to everyone around her, not her. She never discussed dying—why waste the time? Her faith was her shield against pain, sorrow, and fear. She led us on this journey at first with fear of the darkness and then to the light of Christ. She opened our eyes to the power of each moment now and how we can choose to live as Christ tells us: to love God and love our neighbor.

We Are Surrounded by Angelic Souls

And the angel answering said unto him, I am Gabriel that stand in the presence of God, and I was sent to speak unto thee, and to bring thee these good tidings. (Luke 1:19)

So often in the Bible we hear stories of great Christians and their acts of faith. We also learn of the miracles of saints. I believe we also have souls that rise above the challenges in life and strive to bring Christ's love to everyone. I believe in angels among us, sometimes within ordinary people. They are easy to spot in any crowd—gentle and graceful souls with humility we all aspire to, individuals we confide in to help us find our way. They take comfort in helping others. We are surrounded by these gentle souls if we look closely. The souls have a special gift from God—a spirit of love; they are an instrument of God.

Dianne is an angelic soul. You could sense it when you were with her. She struggled with the earthly sins like everyone, but she believed Christ washed away her sins. Dianne's passion was charity in a quiet humble way. She refused to be the center of attention. Dianne did not want sympathy; she was quick to point out others in need facing challenges. What she needed was a chance to share compassion and love.

Dianne actions, especially in her last months, showed us the grace of faith in dying. So often she could replace sorrow with joy with a smile. Dianne showed everyone how to love the moment and how to tie your burden to Christ's Cross and let him carry our burden.

Follow Christ.

> *Through faith you are all children of God in Christ Jesus. For all of you who were baptized in Christ have clothed yourselves with Christ. (Galatians 3:26)*

Christ said "follow me." He didn't say walk with me, or lead me; he said follow me. I was golfing with a gentleman in Maui, and he shared this story with me. He faced cancer and major surgery but believes the prayers of family cured his illness and helped him avoid surgery. So often during Dianne's journey we would hear about how prayers and how Mary's intervention or Christ's intervention was the answer—testimonies of faith that cured major illness or injury. What we discovered is how Christ can use your life as an instrument of good for others. We honor our loved ones by remembering their faith.

Our logical brains often give us thoughts of "why Dianne?" or "why me?". Both are very natural questions that create guilt in us for thinking this way. You cannot avoid it, you feel guilty. But we cannot allow these thoughts to control us. We are sinners but are cleansed by Christ's forgiveness. So often we choose the wrong path but are quickly and gently pulled back by Christ and souls like Dianne. I pray this angelic attitude grows in you. We can be extraordinary if we choose Christ. Our mission is to honor our loved ones, which cannot happen if we are full of sorrow. Redemption is easy, and the path of the righteous is wider when we embrace our faith. I pray Dianne's journey shows us how to live our faith and a better way to remember our departed loved ones. It's easy to remember the good acts of our loved ones who passed away, but Dianne showed us to seek out and nurture the living. Compassion and charity have great rewards on earth.

Seek Comfort from a Priest or Minister

> *Living God, creator of light, grant light to those who call upon you. Open our lips to praise you, our lives to proclaim your love, our work to give you honor and our voices to celebrate you forever. We ask this through Christ the Lord. Amen.*

When Dianne and I faced extremely challenging bad news, we sought comfort from our priest. His blessings and prayers so often helped us learn to trust God. When Dianne learned she would have cancer the rest of her life, our priest came to be with her, bless her, hear her confession, and pray with us. Through his anointing and prayers Dianne was at peace. We so often seek forgiveness, but doubt makes us insecure if we are truly repentant. We learned to always trust our faith whenever fear and uncertainty or other earthly sins crept into our lives. Sometimes we are overly aggressive in our religious actions to make up for insecurities.

After our priest left, Dianne smiled and told me she was blessed that she was free of all her sins. She truly believed she was cleansed.

She passed through the valley of darkness and believed she ready for heaven. An amazing transformation happened at that moment. Her soul was full of the Holy Spirit and visible to everyone who visited her. Although her body was in great pain, her soul was at peace and full of joy.

We witnessed God's presence and love in our home during Mass at our home with the God-teens. Our family priest asked Dianne if he could include the anointing of the sick for Dianne as part of the Mass celebration. Dianne agreed. Everyone felt God's presence during the ointment and Mass especially the young adults who probably had never seen this anointing. For many of us we witnessed how Christ helps the sick and needy. Our priest told everyone this was one his most powerful experiences of Christ's love.

Our priest also organized a home Mass during the last month of Dianne's life. Our home was full of family and friends celebrating Mass together. God's love was with everyone that day, especially Dianne. The anointing was very powerful for everyone. Dianne was fully of joy afterwards making sure to hug or hold hands with everyone. Many friends will talk about how they felt heaven's presence in Dianne. Her smile wiped away our tears.

Our priest was our spiritual guide on the journey, always sharing God's love. Our priest was especially gifted with his Irish wit and wisdom to keep us in the moment and not worrying about the future. I believe his faith added quality to Dianne's life, and maybe more time. He loved Dianne, as everyone else did. Pray for him to find joy and peace.

Celebrate Communion

> *I am the living bread from heaven, says the Lord. Whoever*
> *eats this bread will live forever; the bread I shall give is*
> *my flesh for the life of the world. (John 6:51)*

A friend shared with me how the Eucharist is a mirror for of loved ones to see us and we see them. I agree. I feel her with me today when I receive the Eucharist.

Dianne's journey showed us how the faith of others can strengthen our faith. Dianne loved Mass, but during Dianne's first cancer journey she struggled to find the strength for Mass. Also, big crowds were a challenge because her immune system was so low. Dianne's journey included so many acts of love and faith by friends, priests, and family. We are so grateful for the love and admire their faith.

Because of her love for Mass and her struggle to make it to church, a very close friend asked Dianne if he and some other acolytes from the church could bring communion to Dianne every day. Dianne loved it. Seven men organized together each taking a day of the week to come visit Dianne and bring communion. These spiritual warriors showed their faith in action. The act of communion included prayers, readings, and the sharing of Christ's body. So often the men would visit with her afterwards, and sometimes their wives would join in. I tried to participate most days, but I also recognized how sacred and private this was to Dianne. They never missed a day for the entire journey. When Dianne was cancer free she started back to Mass so the daily communion ended. I know the men missed sharing Christ with Dianne. When Dianne had cancer the second time, the men began the daily communion again without hesitation. And it ended when she was cancer free the second time. Dianne laughed that if she was well enough to go on vacation, she was well enough to go to Mass at church. Dianne's health always improved after communion—she was brighter and livelier. We witnessed the Holy Spirit in our home each time these men share communion with Dianne. When Dianne's cancer returned, so did her heroes. These men brought her communion until the day she passed away.

There are many levels of heroes in the world, and these men are examples of how sharing your faith unselfishly is God using you to help others. They became her spiritual warriors.

Each man will tell you how they benefited more from their actions than Dianne, but Dianne prayed for them because of their acts of love. Each shares their faith and experience:

Jim Essay:

> Upon hearing of Dianne's illness I asked her if it would be okay if I could have some good friends who were Eucharistic ministers, bring Our Lord to her on a daily basis. Without hesitation she said yes. With Msgr. Barr's approval, I recruited six men, and within an hour I had a seven-man team assembled. Each had an assigned day of the week. I can say without reservation that each was extremely humbled to be able to do this for Dianne.
>
> I was the Sunday Eucharistic minister and soon learned what humility truly is. After a few visits, Dianne taught me quickly. It was apparent to me that she knew the undeniable fact that her time on earth was limited but also knew that the Lord Jesus Christ, who she was receiving on daily basis, was sustaining

her. She was being held in his hands and that no matter what happened to her she was safe.

Whatever her daily schedule for treatments or doctor appointments, she would reach out to each of us to coordinate our visit into her daily schedule to make sure that she was able to receive our Lord.

God's love was so apparent and present each time I came to see her. It was a blessing for me to witness her faith, hope, love and incredible perseverance. She was always hoping and praying to get better but knew that regardless it was God's will that would be done.

I humbly thank God that he allowed me the gift of bringing Him in the Holy Eucharist to Dianne. She has been a great witness to me.

Phil Essay:

I have been told that Dianne referred to the men that brought her daily Communion as her "spiritual warriors." More accurately, for over a year, we were Dianne's students. Dianne taught me to live with my eyes open. I know that Dianne believed in a miracle; a cure of her cancer. She got a miracle, all right. It just wasn't what she expected. Dianne's miracle was that her eyes were opened to the power of each and every moment. I remember the day that Dianne's eyes were opened and she accepted God's plan for her. Peace consumed her, and she shared it with everyone around her; the kind of peace that engulfs you, the kind of peace that you could breathe in. Peace. Eyes open to what is important.

Several Tuesdays I arrived at the house with the burden of work and the grind of life weighing heavily on my shoulders. Eyes closed. Dianne was dying of cancer, so I naturally I took notice of Dianne's face, free of burden and worried only about how I was doing that day and every day that I visited thereafter. Eyes open. I asked about what she was eating and drinking and how her last chemotherapy session went. Eyes closed. She wanted to hear the Gospel reading for the day and reflect on how she could comfort me...how she could comfort me. Eyes open. Groups would visit and try to focus everything on Dianne. Eyes closed. Dianne would ask everyone to quiet down and pray the Rosary together. Eyes open. Sometimes praying the Rosary brought her so much peace she would sleep.

Very few times in my life have I had the privilege to be in the presence of another human being with a resolve so strong and clear that you can't help but to follow. Dianne's resolve was to make others her priority. Dianne's body was failing. Physically, she was broken. Spiritually, she was inspiring. Spiritually, she was my warrior. Dianne took evil and turned it into good: the definition of a miracle—Dianne's miracle. Eyes open.

Nick Birkel:

When I think back and reflect on Dianne one word stands out to describe her, and that is strength. When I think about her struggle to fight her awful disease, she was such a fighter with a great attitude and determination to beat this awful disease. She drew on her faith in God and her prayer life to help her in this fight and give her strength to continue. She never complained, nor was she bitter, and she seemed to have a connection with her God, that whatever was in his plan, she could accept. Dianne was always positive that the next treatment or procedure was part of God's plan to give her a cure. Trust—trust in her caregivers and their decisions, trust that her family and friends would always be there, and trust that her God would always be by her side.

One of Dianne's greatest gifts to all of us that knew her, was her example of how we need to continue to grow in our faith and how we need to continue to stay positive and fight our battles and accept what is in God's plan. She was truly an inspiration to me. Many times I felt like after I visited with Dianne, she had given me more with her faith, her fight, her attitude, her determination, her love of God family and friends, her acceptance of God's plan. I felt that she had given me more than I could ever give her. Dianne, thanks for your example, we love you and we miss you.

Chris Raun:

When I look back on my life, I realize that—consciously or unconsciously—I have naturally sought relationships with people who reflect God's love in the world: people who are essentially good; people who are wise; people who are peacemakers; people who care about others; people who are generous with their time; people who in some way inspire hope. Generally speaking, these people don't realize what they do for me, and they don't recognize that I am most likely in their presence at any one moment because I am simply drawn to them. When I encounter these people, I always notice that they are surrounded by other people who are also attracted to them.

Seventeen years ago, I lost a son to brain cancer. At that time, I learned a lot about myself, and I learned a lot about the redemptive nature of suffering. People who suffer in faith reflect God's love in a powerful way and in turn inspire faith in others. My son was stronger than I could have ever imagined in the midst of mental and physical suffering, and God carried him through it by providing all the grace he needed.

The strength suffering people exhibit is proof to me that God offers hope if we simply ask for it. He offered it to me as I watched my son suffer. Witnessing God's freely given grace gives me greater assurance that He is always with us, always listening, always ready to help, removing any shadow of a doubt that He truly loves us and desires to be with us in eternity.

The opportunity I had to share Holy Communion with Dianne on a regular basis would seem an act of charity to a friend undergoing suffering and trial, and it was. However, my act of charity was, in reality, a selfish act. It was selfish because I had so much to gain from her. Delivering the supernatural gift of the Eucharist to Dianne was a great privilege, but witnessing her response to that gift from God and her deep faith during suffering was a wonderful gift to me. Her example through peaceful acceptance of suffering gave witness to God's love, gave me greater hope, and a greater hunger for eternal life with God in heaven.

Norm Goldsmith:

As a Eucharistic minister I have always enjoyed bringing Christ to the sick and those unable to attend mass. In most cases these people are unfamiliar persons or modest relationships. In Dianne's case it was quite different, and I must say, quite special. To have the privilege of bringing the body of Christ to a friend who is terminally ill is beyond words. To hold her hand and pray with her was a very powerful and spiritual encounter with Christ. Dianne was always so grateful to those of us who brought Christ to her, even when she was really sick. She was always so interested in what was going on in my life and never complained about her illness and pain. Through her suffering I was drawn to Christ in a way that I had not known before. We never know how Christ might choose to use each of us to build up His kingdom on earth, but I do know the He was using Dianne to help draw me closer to Him. Until her last months I had only known Dianne socially, but from the very first time we prayed together and she received the body of Christ in the Holy Eucharist, we both knew that Christ was truly present. I will always treasure the honor and blessing to have been chosen as one of the Eucharistic ministers that helped usher our friend Dianne into heaven.

Rick Lange:

I have many sacred memories from my experiences with Dianne and Jim, and I'll share three. The first is a wonderful recollection of me bumping into Jim one evening at the golf practice putting green near their home, which was early on in the time we acolytes were visiting her. I was struck then and still inspired now that he so openly spoke about the power of prayer and reliance on Jesus. It wasn't just an offhand comment but a lengthy sharing by him about the foundation of his and Dianne's existence. Great stuff. I'll call this the gift of authenticity.

Second, Dianne was so welcoming, and I loved that she accepted herself, her health, and all of us just the way we are. I really looked forward to visiting Dianne each week and just becoming one of her friends (she had so many). She was so kind to let me hang out longer than just the Communion time and visit. Who knew that she was such a Packers fan! Now, when I see someone with a Packers' jersey, or a game is on television, I think of Dianne, my friend. I'll call this the gift of friendship.

Third, Jim and Dianne really loved each other, and that was so great to witness. My wife Sue and I have been married thirty-four years now, and I well know how wonderful the Sacrament of marriage can be. I saw Jim and Dianne's relationship as a real living

Sacrament. I'll call this the gift of living out a sacramental marriage.

Bill Stull:

Serving on the altar as an acolyte is one of the greatest honors a person can get. Being there when the consecration takes place putting you just four feet away from our Lord on the altar is an amazing honor. Then distributing the Eucharist to people in church and looking them in the eye brings with it a wide set of emotions. Being ordained an acolyte also enables you to be an Extraordinary Minister of the Eucharist (EME), which allows us to take the Eucharist to people who cannot make it to church.

When I was asked to be a part of the team of men taking the Eucharist to Dianne, I was honored to be asked. As time went on, we were there for her every single day, sharing with her the victories as well as the setbacks. We were taking the Eucharist to her every day to give her some spiritual encouragement and hope. Eventually I realized what a truly courageous and strong woman she was, not letting this cancer get the best of her. Then one day I realized that I was not the one bringing her the strength and hope, but the one receiving it! She was the one being completely optimistic and strong, and she wanted me to feel that before I left. She became an amazing example of what it takes to carry your own cross and not complain. Towards the end, you could just feel the Holy Spirit and angels present when you walked in the door.

Dianne made such a huge impact on my life, which I will never forget. We are praying for you Dianne; please pray for us too. God Bless your soul!

I believe Dianne's life was longer on earth because of communion and these men. God blessed Dianne to have these spiritual warriors in her life, and I encourage anyone on a similar journey to be open to others for help. I also encourage you to be the "hero" in someone's life just like Dianne's seven heroes. Your faith will grow along with theirs.

Open Your Home for Prayer

Remember, O most gracious Virgin Mary that never was it known that anyone who fled to your protection, implored your help, or sought your intercession, was left unaided. Inspired by this confidence, I fly unto you, O Virgin of virgins, my Mother. To you I come; before you I stand sinful and sorrowful. O Mother of the Word

Dianne's friends would come to our house to pray continuously. Organized Rosary sessions also helped her faith grow. Christ tells us that when we gather in his name, he is there. We witnessed his presence in these prayer sessions. So often these friends would kneel around her chair, praying while holding her hand or touching her. Although their intention was to comfort Dianne, each person would share how these prayer sessions helped nurture their souls and strengthen their faith. Dianne loved the time in prayer with her friends. It would be easy to say no or deny the need for it, but Dianne knew how important these sessions were for her friends and how these prayers helped her, too. I believe her hope and optimism grew each time, and I could sense her body being a little stronger.

Let your friends join you on your journey; they will be grateful, and so will you. Dianne's burden was lighter because of her friends.

I was also very moved by the people that asked Dianne to pray for them. They believed she was closer to heaven and could carry their petition to Christ. I knew Dianne was already praying for them, but I could see their comfort in asking for her prayers.

I believe these prayer sessions, the daily communion, the blessings, and prayers with our family priest were Christ at work helping Dianne be at peace during her journey. God blesses us with souls that serve him in prayer.

Be Open for Friends

Behold a wise woman who has built her house. She feared the Lord and walked in the right path. (Proverb 14:1)

Dianne's passion for life and helping others grew stronger during the last years of her journey. Everyone she touched talked about how her transformation changed their lives. So many people wanted to touch her to feel her angelic soul. I often repeat the statement that people would come and see her full of grief or sorrow but leave full of joy and happiness because they witnessed the power of Christ at work in her. Sometimes a gentle touch or a smile from her was all that was needed. Even the nurses in the clinic would often stop and talk with her because she always found a way to make them feel better.

I believe Christ asked her to stay on earth longer than expected. So often the prognosis was not good, yet Dianne would rebound, to the surprise of everyone. Logic would expect the cancer to overcome her nearly two years before she passed away. Dianne's optimism and faith pushed her doctors and nurses to heroic acts. So often when the option was to slow the pain of treatment, Dianne's faith and optimism would persist.

Dianne believed in a miracle and prayed for one constantly. She was convinced a miracle would happen. She wanted to go to Boy's Town one day to pray in the chapel. Father Flannigan may need a miracle to become a saint, so why couldn't Dianne be his miracle? Dianne remembered visiting the chapel when she was very young and on family vacations. She believed this was a place of heaven on earth and would provide her a place to reflect on her faith. I asked her friends to help me take her over, and we all prayed around Father Flannigan and in the chapel. I was always amazed how friends and family would react to any request to share their faith with Dianne. Dianne's miracle did happen— not to her but to everyone around her. Dianne's miracle was her actions that help so many strengthen their faith or even renew their trust in God. I witnessed it at the Boys Town Chapel.

Share Your Love

We can share Christ's love in very easy ways without leaving our comfort zone. A simple random act of kindness is an easy way to start. Dianne and I always loved to buy the order for the car behind us at the drive-thru coffee shop. This simple act changes three people's lives: the person behind you, the drive-thru cashier, and you. You can drive away knowing the positive reaction that is happening because of your simple action. One cashier told me on a later trip that over seven cars paid for the car behind them! She said it was the best day ever for her.

It could be as simple as handing a bottle of water to a homeless person as you walk by. Dianne and I were moved by a speech given by the leader of City Mission who said that if everyone in our city would donate one item from our shelves to the food bank that it would eliminate hunger in our city. Dianne loved organizing our God-teens to collect food for the food bank because we saw the importance this had in the lives of these young adults. We also witnessed the people coming in for food when we delivered the food to the food bank. We were shocked by how young these parents with kids were who needed assistance. Some were the same age as the God-teens. We always left feeling like we didn't do enough.

Christ is giving us ample opportunities to do something simple everyday if we look for it. The next time you are grumpy or feeling down, find a simple act to help someone. I always feel uplifted and thank Christ for reminding me to love our neighbor.

Power of Hope

We can be overly optimistic with a false sense of hope. Dianne's journey shows us how hope can be measured in each day when we do not focus on the outcome but rather the moment. We have a choice to be in misery because of our burden or we can be full of hope. Why not enjoy what we have and not worry about tomorrow? Christ tells us about the lilies of the field so why not let our beauty shine? Dianne's choice inspired us to enjoy the moment. Don't worry, do not be afraid, love life. Hope is a gift from God.

Dianne did not want cancer to define her life; she wanted her life on her terms of hope, compassion, and charity. A close friend shared with me how Dianne did not create the crisis. God knew the plan He had for her life and how she was going to reach out to others. Her friend shares:

> *Dianne wouldn't talk about her dying. That was part of her wisdom. To do so would change the focus to herself and not to others. As long as she focused on others she could go on fighting. And think about our lives, and when we think we want something, it ends up being a letdown. When we focus on doing something for others, it brings energy. Dianne's energy came from not dwelling on herself or her circumstances but rather keeping her focus on God and others. The ripple effect that Dianne's actions will have on people and future generations will be amazing.*

I love the thought! It wasn't just for the present that she wanted to help others through but now and into the future.

Dianne's journey was peaceful and full of joy because of her faith. We can remember our loved ones when we do not focus on their burden but focus on their life. God blessed us with Dianne to show us the way.

Dianne's Blessings

If I Have One More Day on Earth

I will begin the day with a prayer
Thankful for God's love
Thankful for another day
Thankful for my family and friends

I will celebrate my faith
Celebrating Confession
Celebrating Communion
Celebrating lighting a candle for Dianne

I will smile all day
Smiling and Laughing with Friends
Smiling watching children play
Smiling and Singing Joyfully and Loud

I will share Christ's Love
Sharing random kindness
Sharing Compassion for the Hungry
Sharing Hope for the Homeless

I will enjoy every moment
Enjoying the Beauty of the Earth
Enjoying the kindness from helping others
Enjoying every Hug and Kiss

I will close my eyes
Thankful to God for another day
and peacefully journey to heaven.

Journey with Family and Friends

Dianne's journey was shared by her family and friends: A diagnosis that stuns everyone. Everyone feel helpless in the beginning. Each struggles with how to deal with the challenge and how it changes their life. Everyone uncertain what to say or do, often wanting everything to be normal again, hoping to ease Dianne's suffering and their own.

Life changed. No exception. Everything that had been was now going to be different. Even though we attempted to find normalcy, we would not be the same. Each of us had to find peace with the impact to our lives. Dianne would talk about her "new normal" so often, expressing her support to others to ask Christ to help you accept change and find peace.

Dianne had a beautiful family and some amazing friends. Family is often defined by marriage or blood relations, but our "family" also includes close friends we unite with through Christ. They were there to share good times and challenging times. Dianne's journey with family and friends is a journey of "family."

We often focused on Dianne or me or our family, but her journey impacted everyone in our lives. Dianne's friends struggled as much as her family with the journey and her passing away. So often the attention is focused on the family, but friends are suffering as much as her family and need comfort.

Everyone struggles with what to say or do when confronted with Dianne's journey. Our quick responses are heartfelt but create a bigger burden at times if we don't know how to read the signs. We learned what worked well and what was a well-intentioned "oops," but all were acts of love.

For everything there is a season, and a time for every purpose under heaven. (Ecclesiastes 3:1)

We were on the journey of hope for a miracle. Amazingly, on two occasions we celebrated: when Dianne first "beat cancer" with chemo, surgery and radiation. and when she "beat cancer" a second time. Her "family" also struggled each time we learned the cancer was back or worse. This journey became increasingly hard on everyone because her cancer didn't go away. We hugged her, held her hand, and prayed with her for a miracle. Everyone struggled with her journey. We were on the journey together, and all our lives changed. Dianne showed us the way.

I Am Sorry

Dianne heard this phrase repeatedly daily from everybody. Everyone struggles with what to say. Often she would hear "I am sorry" through tears that upset her. What she needed was comfort, not sorrow. What I discovered was Dianne was not upset for herself; she was upset she was creating sorrow in others. This became a heavy burden for her. On top of dealing with learning you have cancer, you also have to confront everyone's sorrow.

A good friend, a priest, reminded me that sorrow is a good thing for our soul. Sorrow helps us remember our love for departed souls. We all feel sorry for anyone with a burden. Dianne's friends and family have grief because they did not want Dianne to have pain. Sorrow does provide comfort for people suffering, so do not be afraid to share your sorrow.

Dianne would rarely talk about her cancer to avoid the sorrow. In fact, so often Dianne would present herself as normal as possible so strangers would not stare and family and friends would feel more comfortable around her. Dianne would laugh and say, "Let me put my head on" before people would come into the house so she would look normal. This was her way of disguising the impacts of cancer. What amazing courage it takes to pretend to be normal. I would work to prepare family and friends before they talked with her. She would add that God has a plan, she would be fine, or she anticipated a miracle. No matter what, she always found a way to comfort them somehow.

Dianne became extraordinary in comforting during the last two years. Her passion was to change their sorrow to joy by reminding them of the blessings we have every day. I believe it was her way of saying there is a time to mourn, and a time to laugh. This is a time to laugh.

Salute one another with a kiss of love. Peace be unto you all that are in Christ (1 Peter 5:14)

Okay, so what is an alternative to say? It is such a trained reaction to say, "I am sorry,." that I find it a challenge to change myself. In truth, we are searching for a way to share our support and love. If these are the emotions we want to share, then why do we express sorrow? I ask everyone, "What would you like to hear?" What is a better way to express our love? Our support?

My best suggestion comes straight from Christ: "Peace be with you." Throughout the Bible we are reminded to share our peace and love. I believe we want our loved one to feel peace and love and know we are there to support their struggles. "Christ's peace be with you" is a reminder that we are not alone. Christ is with us on our journey and with our family and friends, so could this be a better way to express our love?

Christ's blessings be with you. Asking for a blessing for a person in need is a great alternative. Consider a blessing compared to sorrow. A blessing is a request for the future, whereas sorrow is a reaction to the past. We can receive a blessing for a current object or event, so why not ask God to bless our loved one in need? God's blessing is a great act of helping someone in need.

I Will Pray for You; My Prayers Are with You

This is another common response. I find myself repeating it every day. Everyone says it, usually with good intentions. I take everyone at their word and believe them because the power of prayer can bring comfort and miracles. So often I witnessed Dianne's health improve after her friends prayed with her. I believe through prayer Dianne was blessed with many more days of happiness and joy. Believe in the power of prayer and pray.

I asked our priest how he deals with so many requests for prayers. He shared with me how he records the name of people in need in a book, and then he prays and meditates while reading through the book. What a valuable lesson for us all. Find a common time each day in a quiet spot to reflect on our family and friends in need (or not) and pray. Sometimes call out the most in need, but always consider everyone each day. I found as I shared this story that many people do the same thing. What a great idea.

Pray now. "I will pray for you" is an intention, but a good friend reminds us that now is the time to pray. Prayer can comfort our loved ones, so do not be afraid to reach out with a small prayer for blessings and love.

A close friend and I were discussing this one night on the golf practice green. We agreed the need for pray and the power of prayer is very beneficial. But the phrase "I will pray for you" seems flawed. We couldn't come up with an alternative. A few weeks later he came running up to me on the putting green, very excited. He had an alternative: "I will pray with you." What he believed was the slight change in the phrase moves it from a future to a current tense. So often another close friend I would call would always ask to pray with me on the call. What a powerful tool to have—multiple people praying at the same time for our loved one. Our faith tells us that whenever two or more gather in his name, Christ is with us. On many occasions Dianne was very fatigued, barely able to sit up or stay awake. However, every time someone would ask to pray with her, she was very attentive, and I believe she became more alert. The people who came to pray the rosary with her would laugh because she so often would doze off during the rosary but always said amen at the right time.

Pray. I witnessed so often a calming effect on Dianne when people prayed. We could feel God's presence, and it helped deal with the daily challenges.

Everyone Has a Story

Dianne listened with love to many stories from people who talked about someone who beat cancer or died from cancer. Maybe the intention was to comfort her, but I never understood how. Maybe they were trying to say someone else beat cancer. It seemed to me the story teller was trying to change the focus away from Dianne's story, a way of avoiding the issue. I never really understood the need to tell Dianne or her family these stories. I understand the story teller is dealing with a loss of a loved one and needed the sympathy.

Dianne was quick to offer comfort, but I am not sure how. Dianne would scold me when I would comment in private. She reminded me of their need for support dealing with their grief. She believed her burden reminded them of another loved one. Maybe they were trying to deflect sympathy on to themselves but so what? She was right. We all need support, but I do think we should try and find a way to share our story in a supportive way by focusing on how it will improve the person's struggle.

For example, we learned many tips for dealing with side effects or alternatives to treatments and ideas on what to eat or drink. Share your love and your life experiences to help the person with a burden. God will increase his love for you as you share your love.

My daughter Julie always says that everyone has a story similar to Dianne's, so you cannot judge anyone.

Being a good listener is a great alternative if you do not know what to do. God is also working in your presence as much as the words you say.

What Can I Do?

Society has taught us to react with acts of kindness, of love. We need to do something: bring food, offer prayers, help with house-keeping or yardwork. We feel helpless when someone is in pain. We want to ease their burden. What we are doing are expressions of love and support. From the day we found out Dianne had cancer, the acts of kindness began. Someone immediately helped clean the house. Every day we received gifts of food, incredibly delicious food. The time and talent that is needed to prepare this food is so obvious. Dianne and I would laugh because we never had home cooking that was so good.

Timing is a big challenge for acts of kindness. I share this as a reminder to consider the condition of your loved one. Dianne treated every act with love in return. I learned so much about grace and humility when I watched her hug and share a tear of joy with people who brought her food and other gifts.

However, on occasion the food became a burden. Dianne would help me greet and thank someone who brought us food. She would hug and talk with them. However, no sooner did they leave and she would need the food taken away, far away. She was nauseated by the smells. I witnessed her immediately becoming sick. Chemo and radiation messed up her sense of smell and taste. She would try to eat but couldn't. No matter how much love went into preparing the food, Dianne could not enjoy the love. This upset her because she wanted to genuinely be grateful but could not truthfully talk about her enjoyment. These gifts were a blessing for me, but often I sat on the patio to enjoy them. She didn't like being the center of attention, but she appreciated the expressions of love.

I am not suggesting that you not bring food to those in need; I strongly encourage it. I am suggesting that you consider timing. If your loved one is in chemo or radiation struggling with side effects, then consider another act of love and support.

I asked our priest this question once and he was quick to say the best act of kindness is presence as a listener. I agree. Dianne spent an incredible amount of time with nothing to do. She didn't have the strength for her daily activities and often was unable to drive herself. Her day mostly consisted of sitting in a chair watching her favorite daytime shows and napping. Dianne loved to read but even reading became a struggle. Social media allowed her to stay current with family and friends. Highlights of her day were when anyone came to visit. Even if she was fatigued, she did not pass on a chance to see friends. Just a simple visit was a great act of kindness, and my first answer when people asked, "What can I do?" was "Come visit."

Again, timing is critical. The first time she had cancer she was very guarded and often did not like to see people. She did know how to cope with the questions. She would dismiss her medical procedures as being much easier than they actually were so she could avoid sympathy. She wanted to feel normal again. Dianne and I had long talks on how others needed to help more than she was willing to believe she needed. She would talk about how the act of helping was important for them to deal with Dianne's journey. Dianne resolved to always embrace any act of love.

She Is in a Better Place

Dianne was an instrument of God to show us the way, to teach us how to live each moment. We often are reminded that Dianne is in heaven and no longer in pain. What a beautiful sentiment.

It is a good reminder of God's plan. The comment also reminds us that Dianne lived a Christ-centered life. People also like to remind us that Dianne is with us always. She is watching.

Sometimes I think we say this when we do not know what to say. I hear it often when I reflect on how I miss her or that she would have enjoyed the moment or event. I feel the sense of loss most when we are with family at an event that Dianne would enjoy: a friend's concert, a social gathering, a football game, but most often at Mass. Dianne so loved to celebrated Mass that I cannot help but tear up during Mass, especially the Eucharist. A reminder she is in heaven is a wonderful sentiment.

I experience these moments every day, and I think this is healthy. Yes, I feel some grief, but it is overwhelmed by my wish for Dianne to be there for her enjoyment. My tears are not for me, but for how I know she would have loved the moment. I am confident this is a very common emotion by everyone. We wish for joy and happiness on earth for our loved one even though we know they have eternal joy and happiness in heaven. I guess we are selfish like that, but I think it is okay. In fact, I think remembering our loved one helps us enjoy the moment more.

I also laugh because I thought she had it pretty good here on earth. She always was happy. But I know heaven will be beautiful, so I cannot be too selfish.

Do Not Be Afraid

So often people were reluctant to stop by the house and see her but left believing it was the best thing for Dianne and themselves. People would often stop by, crying and afraid. They confided in me they were afraid to see her sick or dying. They wanted to remember her when she was normal. I understand the fear.

Dianne found a way to change every visit into hope, optimism, and strengthening faith. Short visits became increasing longer, and more people came to visit. Consider avoiding the time after each treatment. Do not feel obligated to bring anything. Your time is the greatest expression of love. An unexpected treat is appreciated, like a milkshake or favorite snack, something you can share with your loved one. Consider taking them out to lunch. What a great time and a break for the care giver.

Ask questions. So often Dianne was asked, "How do you feel?" This is a tough question to answer. Consider how you would answer the question if you were Dianne. You constantly have bone pain, your immune system is intentionally weak causing you to be nauseous, you're tired, and struggle to focus. Dianne would smile and tell you she was okay or laugh about her chemo brain or her body having "one of those days." Do not be afraid to learn about the cancer and treatments.

A couple that were very close friends of ours shared a similar journey when their son passed away from brain cancer. They shared with me an afternoon when their son's friends were visiting. Someone asked him how he was and the room was quiet for a few minutes followed by their son explaining the treatments but avoiding the question asked. They were so proud of his heroic efforts to comfort his friends in his answer.

My suggestion is to ask questions about the procedures and the process but try to avoid questions on severity of pain and side effects. Dianne easily discussed the process as long as the conversation did not turn to sadness or sorrow. Dianne never gave up hope, so these emotions often showed her others were not as optimistic. Dianne was a classic example of Mohammed Ali's famous quote: "If a mosquito thinks it can pull a plow, hitch it up and get out of the way," a great analogy of Dianne's hope, maybe even a little understated.

She would confide to a point but rarely open up about the pain and suffering and the daily challenges she faced. She would scold me if I started to talk about it with friends. Dianne knew the sorrow people would have if they really understood what she was going through. She made no complaints or even the slightest hint of a complaint. Dianne's oncologist told me during visitation at the mortuary that Dianne was the only patient in his career who never complained.

A Simple Card

Consider how powerful a simple greeting card with your expressions of support and love will mean to someone in crisis. I didn't expect the volume of get-well cards and how much strength she found in these random acts of kindness. We knew that Christ was involved when she received a card on a challenging or painful day. I would see her read it several times. Some cards became very private to her. The sentiment of the printed words was inspirational, but Dianne found the greatest comfort in the few lines written by her friends.

Equally, I learned how powerful the sympathy cards were for our family after she passed away. I received some amazing cards and letters. I also found comfort and love in the handwritten words added to each card.

These acts of love remind us to thank Christ for our family while they are living and not when they are in heaven. Several of the sympathy cards reflect thoughts the person wanted to share with Dianne before she passed away. Dianne needed the love, and so did the individual. Take time to share your love with the living. This taught me a lesson to find time to reach out to others more than I used to because I learned how this simple act was so important.

I share some examples from cards at the end of this chapter as a tribute to Dianne and how she impacted others. The cards are inspirational even today. I was very grateful for the thoughts on Dianne, especially how Dianne impacted their lives. These are great examples if you also find yourself at a loss for words next time you are writing a simple card.

Give Your Guilt to Christ

Guilt is often our first reaction is for our loved one, but we each struggle with how it will impact us. What if I lose a mother, or sister, or friend? This is a very natural reaction. How will my life change if she dies? Our faith guides us with prayers for our loved one and expressions of love in support. But we really have to look for answers on how to be supportive for ourselves.

We also struggle with whether we did enough. Was I there enough? Should I have done more? Should we have done more things she wanted to do in life? Many friends often tell me they wish they would have done more or spent more time with her. They struggle with this guilt and still do.

I forced myself to not think about her dying while she was alive. I would catch myself in dreams wondering what I would do. My inner voice of Christ talking to me reminded me to stop worrying and enjoy the moment. God has a plan. I created an exercise whenever this doubt crept into my brain. I would pray our Lord's Prayer over and over until I went back to sleep. Or, I would theoretically pose the question to Dianne and see what played out in my brain. I recommend this approach if you are helping someone who is dying. You will hear Christ in your inner voice and find peace quickly. Or, I would pray a rosary asking for forgiveness and relief from these thoughts. Do not feel guilty, but I prayed I also reconcile that I gave Dianne great love in every deed I did, in every prayer. I found an inner peace with Christ knowing I did improve Dianne's life on earth. I remembered Dianne lived a life of joy and happiness because of me.

Christ's peace be with you.

Excerpts from Cards of Support and Comfort

We are praying for you and thinking of the blessings God gave you with Dianne. Those memories will last an eternity.

I pray that God wraps his loving arms around you.

Boys Town meant a lot to me the day we went there with Dianne, I will never forget it! (This writer helped Dianne and friends go to the chapel at Boys Town to pray.) although we did not know Dianne well, we considered her a great friend, neighbor and fellow Cornhusker fan....

Remembering Dianne in her beautiful, unselfish, amazing way. She is a great example for all of us in every way of her life. We Mixed Bags will miss her dearly. We will pray for Dianne because praying for a friend is part of being a friend.... (Mixed Bags was one of Dianne's book clubs.)

I will always treasure the time spent in prayer with Dianne. Can't thank you enough for graciously opening your home to us. I know I felt a teeny, teeny bit of heaven in your family room, what a gift

We will always remember her friendly smile and love of life

It is with great sadness we mourn Dianne's death. She fought a courageous, always positive fight against her cancer…and she is now wrapped in His loving arms free of any pain. It was an honor to know Dianne for so many years. Her passing leaves a void in this world

Though we are not friends, we share many mutual friends who have shared your wife Dianne's courageous journey with cancer. I am so very sorry to hear Dianne passed away far too young. I know your pain first hand having lost my husband nearly four months ago. I pray for you and your family. Be kind to yourself

Thank you for including us in Dianne's journey

We enjoyed her friendship so much and will miss her deeply

We will miss your beautiful wife and mom. She was so special to so many people. We were blessed to call her a friend

Throughout high school, she was such a good friend and always there to listen and ready to have a good time. She made me feel good about myself when I needed a lift. I will always remember her special smile and prayers

She was one of the most courageous people that I have ever known and the passion with which she fought her cancer was unsurpassed...we think of her often and will cherish our fond memories of Dianne from the client conferences and especially the inaugural Michigan/Nebraska football game

Dianne was so easy to get to know, we will miss her everyday

I have fond memories of Dianne from all the times we got together when our kids were so young

We can be comforted by knowing Dianne is in our Lord's arms praying for us

I am so sorry for the passing of the beautiful soul that is Dianne. I have learned so much from her over these many years, about life and love and grace

May the memories of Dianne that you cherish bring you strength and comfort in this time of sorrow

Dianne has been my sweet friend where we shared the common bonds of being a wife, mother, sibling and friend. The most desirable trait of a good friend is an accessible ear

Dianne was an inspiration and fought a courageous battle

Dianne is one more reason to look forward to Heaven for us. we hold our memories of our times together. May her love give you strength

We are so honored to have been there to wish Dianne on her way to heaven. Her kindness to us will never be forgotten. She will truly be loved by all and we miss seeing her smiling face

One of my fondest memories of Dianne is the day I ran in to her. she was buying a new pair of shoes on her way to the airport to fly out to meet you. A woman after my own heart

Home at Last
We are all God's children
From the morning hour of birth
He lets us live and laugh and love
And have our day on earth
He guards us through the afternoon
Till sunsets' rays are cast
Then, one by one, with gentle words
He calls us home at last.
-Phyllis Culp Mabry

Dianne was such a bright light to all that knew her

Dianne was always so happy and made everyone fill welcomed. She will be missed

Dianne was an amazing woman

What a joy it was to know Dianne! She was a special "child of God." May our dear Lord continue to bless you

Comfort in knowing what a great role model she was

...I will always treasure all of our frivolity—her memory lives on in me every day with Dianne's continued gift of listening, prayers, friendship—she was my constant compass...

The day I got to meet Dianne – she came to pick up Morgan and we chatted for a half hour. And I thought how wonderful it was to have such a great aunt. And for the next 10 years I found out how wonderful it was for everyone who knew her...her legacy lives on every time we cheer on the Huskers and take time to enjoy all life has to offer—because that is what she taught us all

Dianne was a beautiful soul, she had a kind and gentle spirit

I am honored that I shared many great memories with Dianne on the golf course. She was a genuine loving and caring individual that would do anything for others. May her memories continue to bless each one of you

Dianne was such a kind, generous spirit and we always enjoyed time with her at baseball games and family events

I got to know Dianne through my good friend. We all exercised together–Dianne was always fun, upbeat, a true joy to be around! She made our world a better place and her sparkle will live on

Our hearts hurt with you and yet we smile as we think of Dianne walking with Jesus

Heaven just got a little brighter! What a beautiful woman she was What a blessing Dianne was to all the God Teens to help them grow in their faith and love of God

Dianne was a beautiful person loved by so many

I wish I would have had the opportunity to know Dianne as I heard so many great things about her

We admired you both from afar as you and Dianne handled yourselves with such grace, courage and dignity

Dianne touched so many people and her spirit lives on in all of them

She was a wonderful, courageous woman of faith. I will continue to pray for her…and I will offer a Mass for the repose of Dianne's soul. May the peace of Christ which is beyond understanding be with you-(from a priest)

What no eye has seen, nor ear heard, nor the heart of man imagined what God has prepared for those who love him

Dianne was a beautiful person inside and out. I had the pleasure of being acquainted with her during the time I worked with Julie. Dianne had a knack of making you feel welcome. She will truly be missed for her convivial spirit

From the little I know about the years since Dianne's diagnosis, I admired the fact you savored each moment with each other and truly maximized the remaining time

Dianne was my second mom and such an incredible role model for the type of mother that I wanted to be

Looking back I see that you were a full participant in what I believe is the greatest fight I may see during my lifetime. Years ago, when Dianne first learned of her predicament, I sensed that she was so emotionally overloaded that she would quickly surrender. But instead, I believe she put on the most incredible fight for her life and for her right to live it as she thought it should be lived. She faced setback after setback and kept coming back and living like she was "supposed to"

I apologize for not telling you and Dianne how much I appreciated everything you two did for me. I was probably the most quiet person in our God Teens group, but I truly did value every moment spent with you, Dianne, and the rest of the gang. Being part of something as great as our God Teens group is an honor. I was pretty shy, but I always felt safe and comfortable during our meetings. My relationship with God grew greater than I thought possible. Thank you for keeping me strong in my faith. I know that if I hadn't met you and Dianne, I would be a completely different person. I wasn't very open about my personal problems, but I got through them because of you and Dianne. You two reminded me that anything is possible with God. I have not taken off the Gabriel Necklace since I received it, and I will cherish it forever. Every time I notice it I think of how loved I really am. Thank you for teaching me the greatest lesson of my life! How to Love. I will continue to pray for you and Dianne, I look forward to seeing you both in paradise someday...(Dianne gave each God-teen a Gabriel medal on a chain for high school graduation)

Dianne's Blessings

Journey with My Friend

Fear thou not; for I am with thee: be not dismayed; for I am thy God: I will strengthen thee; yea, I will help thee; yea, I will uphold thee with the right hand of my righteousness. (Isaiah 41:10)

God blessed me with Dianne in marriage. We share a single soul, united by God. Place your hands with palms together and fingers outstretched as in prayer. Your hands mirror each other, different but made to unite as one, just as a man and woman. Marriage combines the two into one in prayer. Each finger represents a gift of love for each other. Now, fold your fingers interlocking. This is God's marriage for Dianne and me. Then, it is very hard to tell which finger belongs to each hand, which gift comes from each other.

God gave us a path for marriage that last for almost thirty-seven years. Dianne and I only dated a few months before we decided to marry. Her friends thought she was crazy. God had a plan for us, a path easy and full of love because of our faith. We didn't worship at the same church, but we had common beliefs. My love and life with Dianne could fill a book. And there is no easy way to sum it up, so I will not try.

Marriage Is Caregiving

Dianne's gifts of love for me included wife, mother, faith guide, cooking, bookkeeping, and household, while always gently reminding me of my strengths: my gifts as husband, father, protector, and wage earner, always in support of Dianne. She knew I was as passionate about my job as she was about charity, so she tolerated my long hours and being missing at critical times.

Trust grows in marriage as we learn to recognize our efforts as gifts of love. Our faith and devotion for each other grows when we accept these gifts without questioning how our partner does it and learning to not demand recognition for our gifts. Our love grew as we learned to accept without criticism the gifts from each other.

Caregiving is commonly a reference to "helping another individual with an impairment with his or her activities of daily living." I didn't believe I was a caregiver for Dianne; we were changing our gifts of love for each other.

One of the great challenges of caregiving is being a loving partner and a caregiver.

My friends would often wonder how I did it and whether they could, but I am convinced they could. It is easier because of our love and devotion in marriage. I admit there were times I struggled, but I asked Christ to help me, and he always showed me the way. I know my friends would do the same if necessary.

I quickly learned to consider her first always, in everything I did. That is easy to believe but impossible to do, creating guilt.

No can prepare you for the challenge. I lived expecting Dianne to always take care of me and outlive me. I made the mistake one day with a close friend of commenting on how I wished it was me and not her with the burden. This was a friend who also had cancer and whose wife passed away from cancer. He became extremely upset with me, telling me how selfish I was thinking. He was right.

Dianne needed me to support her on her journey, not think about myself. This is God's plan for her, and she needed support. I understand the anguish of people in my position. You want the best for your loved one, you do not want them to suffer, and you want them happy and pain free. You constantly pray for these hopes. I was inspired by Dianne. Yes, she wanted to be cancer free, but she was resolved not to waste energy on worrying about death or complaining about the pain. Her faith showed forth with a gentle smile and words of Christ's love.

Temporary Changes in Our Gifts

One of the great lessons I learned in caregiving is never, never, never make your loved one feel guilty because of what you are doing.

Dianne's journey shifted our gifts of love. When she started chemo and radiation she lacked the strength to do much of her daily routine. This created guilt for her because she didn't like being a burden. I had to learn to do these things without complaint so I could ease her guilt.

I lacked basic housekeeping skills. She had to teach me how to run the dishwasher, washer, dryer, and all the appliances. She tried to show me how to hold up the dishwasher door while latching and then turn the knob to wash. Where is the LED panel? Where are the gadgets? I laughed because after the quick tutorial, I went and bought new appliances. I need gadgets. She tolerated these changes but understood my geekiness.

Prior to Dianne's journey I was banned from the grocery store because I always came home with too much random stuff and too many snacks. Many humorous stories were the result of my grocery shopping. The first chemo treatment I went to the store to stock up for the weekend. Dianne gave me a list. I must have looked lost when a young girl asked if she could help me. I handed her my list and followed her around the store. This trip last two hours. During her next chemo treatment, she texted me the list in order of the aisles. this was good except I went to the wrong store. Thanks to another friendly clerk I was on time to pick her up. Traditionally Dianne went to the grocery store every few days. My plan was to make one trip a week. When I got home and proudly showed her my purchases, she gently reminded me we lacked freezer space for all that food. She was patient in her teachings and accepted this as temporary. Later in her journey I could tell she was training me for the future.

Cooking was a challenge for both of us. Dianne did have a few special meals that she would make, but we ate out often for a reason. This became a real challenge when she was struggling, but so often family helped.

I could not figure out the organization of the kitchen. What was in each cabinet? It never made sense to me, but it was her domain and not for me to criticized. We are both different in problem solving; I very logical in organization, Dianne very subjective. She knew where everything was because she put it there and remembered.

I reorganized the cabinets my way. This is one of the biggest mistakes I made as a caregiver. Although Dianne never complained, I realized that I was taking away her gift, reducing her contribution to the marriage. It also became a silent message saying I don't think you will be able to do this again, a message that said I can do it without you. I know Christ was talking to me when I made this realization. I needed Dianne to remain engaged and in charge of her gifts and realized I was only temporary until she could do it again.

Struggling Chef

One of the big challenges of caregiving is helping your loved one keep up their strength by finding something for Dianne to eat that didn't make her sick. I was amazed how random taste and smells changed. So often I failed. We attempted advice from the cancer center staff. Her weight loss and lack of strength were a concern. She would need fluids or blood to keep her strength up and prevent postponing treatments. There is no easy answer. I learned to be patient when my efforts did not work. I reminded myself that she did not want to be in this situation, and I need to work the problem. She wanted to eat normally but her body refused the food. I also learned that anything I ate that had smells could make her sick. I ate a lot of meals on the patio.

The pantry started looking like the beverage aisle at the store. I kept on hand multiple beverages including protein drinks, sodas, juices, teas—anything that she might be able to drink. I found clear beverages tend to be safer such as ginger ale, Sprite, Fresca, and unflavored teas. Sports drinks helped. Sometimes milkshakes helped. I needed to be prepared because there were times water tasted like metal, and she needed something to stay hydrated.

Any nutritional support is a great benefit. Do not be afraid to experiment. I also learned how to advise friends on what to bring when they wanted to help.

We learned how to mask her challenge when we would go out to eat with friends. She would often order and pick at it, taking home most of the meal but happy to be able to spend time with others. I think she did it to give me a break. God love her spirit to battle through these challenges. I wish we could find a better way to help our loved ones keep up their strength.

Controlling the Purse Strings

Dianne knew every nickel burned a hole in my pocket, so I managed the investments, and she paid our bills. I didn't realize was the additional burden on Dianne was hidden in the bill paying. Not only did she have to deal with our household bills but she also had to deal with all the medical bills. The household was not a problem. She hated the burden that her journey created for us.

The cost of cancer is extraordinary even when you have good insurance and the support we received from my company. The deductibles, the out-of-plan costs, our share of the bills, and especially the optional expenses were enormous. I do not understand how anyone can handle it without medical insurance. The cancer center was amazing with an advocacy program to help. The health insurance company was helpful. I wish the hospitals would learn from these groups. So often we would get a bill for the entire treatment from the hospital and it was up to us to pay it or get the insurance company to pay. This never happened with the cancer center. Dianne didn't like to talk about it, even with me, and often would question if she needed a treatment because of the money. My mistake was my neglect to take this burden from her so she didn't feel bad about the cost. I didn't realize this problem until late in her journey. She needed to be focused on getting better, not how to pay for it. She often refused my efforts to buy her things to help her feel better because she didn't want me to spend my money that way. My money. When did our money become mine? I think when she learned she would have cancer the rest of her life is when she changed. There are many mistakes I made during her journey that I would do differently today. This is top of the list. She deserved better.

The Most Beautiful Woman on Earth

Dianne has the bluest eyes I have ever seen and a smile that made you smile to be near her. Her pale skin offset by her beautiful dark brown hair is rare beauty. God gave to me a beautiful wife that I always cherish.

I learned to continue seeing her beauty as the cancer changed her physically. Dianne became very insecure about her appearance during her journey. She struggled with the permanent loss of hair. She would rush to "put her head on" whenever around anyone until the last few weeks of her life. She struggled with the radiation burns that scarred her from the beginning as well as the impact of the mastectomy. Our love was so personal that it didn't change my attraction to her. I think God showed me how to continue to see her beauty improve. We all have a perfect image of ourselves we want to see and often struggle when we don't match that image. I do understand why marriages become challenged when physical changes happen. I actually believe our love was stronger because of the changes. I know God was helping us to continue seeing the beauty in each other.

I struggled helping Dianne feel good about her changes. I am sure I told her how beautiful she was too many times. But I meant it. This was a challenge of the journey: not my feelings for her but her feelings for herself.

Dianne loved to shop and have beautiful clothes, especially shoes. During the last years of her journey she rarely would buy new clothes. The challenge with shoes was how swollen her feet became and the constant blistering caused by the chemo. The weight changes also impacted her clothes. She often said she didn't want me to spend the money on her. She would laugh and tell me that she would grow back into her clothes but I think there was more to it than that.

I believe we all have a picture of how we will look in heaven. I know she is happy in heaven because she has hair again and no burns. My vision for Dianne is as beautiful as she was the day she passed away.

Nurturing Her Spirit

Dianne remained faithful and loving to God all her life. She had the strength we all needed for her journey. I counted on Dianne to show me what to do. She knew when I was struggling and could quickly pull me closer to peace. I tried to hide my fears and grief and remain optimistic. Christ helped me many times when I felt helpless and needed to be strong.

We often used laughter to see us through tough times. When she fell one day and I was picking her up, she told me I needed to get into shape. She saw my anguish and made us laugh. On another occasion when I was helping her up out of a chair, I had her put her arms around my neck. As I was lifting her. I asked her if she was making a pass at me and she laughed and said "you would know it if I was."

Whenever she was discouraged, I made sure her devotion to Christ was there. Her family and our family priest were always available. I hope I did everything I could to help her pray and celebrate her faith.

My sorrow was overwhelming when I witnessed her comforting her friends and family. I knew I needed to be strong for them as well and tried offering comfort. I found myself nightly crying after she fell asleep as I thought about her last visits with family. I couldn't help feeling sorrow for their suffering.

Dianne gave me everything, especially love. I hope she leads me by the hand to heaven someday.

Guilt

Guilt came from many sources—worrying if I did enough, for thinking about life after she passed away, for complaining about doing her duties, worrying whether I was there enough, and feelings of selfishness when she needed support. My struggle with guilt continues. Christ is still helping me.

These are natural human feelings, but I felt guilty because I felt self-centered when she needed me. I forced myself to pray whenever these thoughts entered my head. Prayer gave me something to focus on until these thoughts went away. Whenever I would wake from a dream about the future, I would go into prayer so I didn't think about it. I noticed I didn't dream after she passed away. I struggled, thinking about the future alone. This has to be a common grieving process whenever a loved one passes away. I am afraid to dream because what if she is in my dream or not in my dream? How can I dream without sadness? A friend whose wife passed away a year earlier told me to be patient with myself, that he experiences the same challenge. Praying helps me during these nights.

I am understanding when her friends and family share their guilt with me for not spending more time with Dianne. I feel guilty when I think I did everything she asked, but what about the things she wanted that she never told me? I smile when anyone always tells me what Dianne confided in them that I never knew.

Whenever I struggle with guilt, I think about what Dianne would say or do. I visualize her gentle smile, and my guilt goes away. I ask Christ for his mercy and forgiveness, and trust the thoughts he tells me that I did okay and have peace.

A few friends ask me if I have seen any signs from Dianne. One friend told me how her mother recently passed away and she was struggling with loss. A white dove appeared to her at the cemetery, where she had never seen doves before. She noticed it following her car as she left. She realized it was her mother saying she is at peace. She continues to see the doves and knows it is a sign from her mother.

A taxi driver told me of a tragic accident that took her husband's life. She often wondered why he died and she survived. She also talked about signs she sees that tell her to be at peace and trust in Christ.

I shared earlier my experience when I saw Dianne in the casket for the first time. How quickly all my sorrow changed to joy because I could see her beauty and peace. One of Dianne's closest friends also shared a similar experience after the loss of a loved one.

Take Care of Yourself

I heard this phrase very often, and I appreciate the sentiment. I rarely had a full night's sleep for most of the last year of Dianne's life. Julie would remind me this is the life of every mother of a newborn. I took advantage of a few business trips to sleep all night, but after her seizure she wanted me to be with her. Her day was resting in a chair, so I experimented with different zero gravity chairs to help her sleep better. At nights I slept on the couch nearby so I could hear her when she needed help. One night, while putting away the laundry, I fell asleep in the bedroom, only to be awakened by my phone ringing. It was Dianne needing help. She had called out to me for over an hour and couldn't wake me. We laughed so often about where I would doze off. I bought a baby monitor so that didn't happen again. Most of her moving around required a walker or a wheelchair. Friends helped build handrails and ramps when she no longer could step up a few stairs.

She needed me to monitor her medication because there was a lot of it, and her chemo brain would get confused. The pharmacy would make fun of my labels because I would add a label identifying what it was in our terms instead of the medical names. It worked because of our teamwork.

Her naps gave me time to keep up with my job. My company was incredibly supportive working around my schedule and video conferencing instead of having in-person meetings. Having a virtual office also allowed me to stay current and work while she was in treatments. I don't think the cancer center ever saw me without the laptop open. Maybe I was hiding behind it when she received her "head shots."

I am not sure how I could have received help for any of these things and maintained her privacy and dignity. Maybe it is me being selfish in wanting to spend more time with her.

I worried every day that she might not wake. I would check to see if she was breathing, unsure what I would do if she wasn't. Her last hospital visit made this worse when they told me what was likely to happen. I worried all the time. Each breath was a struggle, but I saw it as a gift from her and was grateful. I know she loves me for what I did, even when I did it wrong. We found a way to laugh at our mistakes, and we laughed a lot. Her love was all the motivation I needed.

Daily Inspiration

I am more aware of others on similar journeys and inspired by their spirit: Friends who daily care for loved ones for decades. A good friend who assists a husband after a terrible accident. She continues to share amazing courage daily and still found time to comfort Dianne. You can see her angelic soul when you see the loving and tender way she cares for her husband every day. Christ's love in her new normal life is an unmistakable aura of holiness.

I watch the love of parents dealing with children with lifelong burdens and see their faith and love in action. These angelic souls inspired me to never be discouraged and always to do more than what Dianne needed.

Living Alone

I miss her. I think about her every day. I appreciate my friends who put up with me constantly talking about her. I cannot help it; I have done it for thirty-seven years, and it is a habit I love. I find great comfort in knowing she is in heaven. I smile when I know she is no longer in pain. But I feel my loss daily.

I get comfort in visiting her at the cemetery and praying a Rosary. I go there whenever I feel sadness and leave rejoicing that she is with Christ in heaven.

It hits me often at the strangest times. One day I borrowed the soap from her bathroom sink and then realized I didn't have to put it back.

It really hits me when I am out with friends and realize how much Dianne would have loved to be there. I miss her commentary afterwards. I do not want to burden others who are also dealing with her not being here, so I find it better to slip away. I feel loved by everyone and not pitied, but I cannot always be sad when I think about the good time she is missing.

I struggle at night when I usually recounted my day's highs and lows. I do not have anyone I can share my successes with who will listen with love. I also miss hearing her highs and lows. She and I loved our God-teen meetings that we started with Highs and Lows. Often the lows were homework, but on occasion we shared intimate challenges with each other and found comfort in the group.

I do not feel that I am alone because she is always in my thoughts. God joined our souls for eternity. Our soul is now half in heaven with Dianne and half on earth with me, Dianne was angelic in her caring for others, and I know she is still that way even in heaven. I pray that someday I will be with her in heaven.

Five Conversations
with Dianne

There are five conversations I would like to have with Dianne. We talked about our dreams, plans, budget, family, and faith. We were not shy in communicating issues and listening to each other's opinion.

In our marriage, it was always difficult to tell who made decisions because we discussed everything. We had so much love and trust that we depended on each other. I laugh when I think about how many times Dianne let me decide, or so I thought. Our partnership depended on the contributions we each made without question. Many times we would discuss, pray, and consider our choices over time, but Dianne knew she who she was dealing with, and also I knew she trusted me even when I made poor choices. After Dianne passed away, I found myself searching for a decision on a matter we typically decided together. I have peace of mind knowing I am doing the right thing and that Dianne will love what I do. I know that Christ is guiding my thoughts and actions. Family and friends also reassure me I am doing the right thing. However, as I face each of these challenges, I reflect on how easy it was to have these discussions before she passed away. I am also amazed at how complex the answers can be when faced with making the decision alone. I am surprised by the burden I would have left her if I passed away first. I am sure she would struggle just as I am. Our marriage and love was strongest when we focused on reducing the burden for each other. My simple wish is that we found the time to have these simple conversations.

I share this reflection with a prayer that you will find the time for these conversations with your loved ones. Everyone is afraid of dying, so often we do not want to talk about it. This prayer is for you to share your love by easing their burden when you die. This is an act of love, not fear.

I shared drafts of these conversations with many friends to hear their perspectives. At first we all believe we have it under control, but as we consider each of the conversations we realize what we missed and how easy and joyful these conversations could be. I also laugh and add that if you don't have these conversations, then die first.

1. How Do You Want to Be Remembered?

Dianne and I never really discussed how we wanted to be remembered. We didn't discuss much about funeral arrangements, either. After Dianne passed away, I asked the question of many friends and family about both Dianne and themselves. I hadn't really even considered it much myself before she passed away. I was surprised by the monetary gifts given in Dianne's honor. The challenge became what to do with the money.

I feel an urgency to create an inspirational memorial to Dianne that will continue her legacy. The question of a memorial involves a search for what is the best way to remember this extraordinary Catholic. This is a mission I do not take lightly and wish for her wisdom on what I should do. I continuously pray for the guidance to find a way to continue sharing her life story and her beliefs. I search for a way for her life to continue to be an inspiration. I would love to have a short conversation with her and listen to what she wants and make sure I commit to it the rest of my life.

Each of us can be remember in memories (in our thoughts), helping others (in our actions), and some form of memorial (in our deeds).

In Our Thoughts

Everyone wants to be remembered for their faith, charity, kindness, actions, and their family and friends. This also defines our uniqueness and faith. Many people say that being remembered by family and friends is good enough. Dianne's close friend says that we create a heart print on our loved ones that will never go away. This is the greatest way for each of us to be remembered.

Dianne was a great inspiration of faith, love, family, and marriage to everyone who knew her. Her friends shared with our family how she changed their lives. I witnessed many occasions where Dianne's faith changed people lives. I have so many cards and letters as well as personal conversations with people who shared how Dianne changed their life and made their faith stronger. So often people shared moments when they were with Dianne and felt an "angelic experience." There are very personal testimonies of how they aspire to be like Dianne. Our memories of Dianne will include her need to serve others, not to be served. She did not like attention on her; she wanted to share Christ's love. In our lifetime we each are blessed to meet angelic individuals so inspirational that you can see and tell how they change lives, how they make us all want to be a better friend, family member, and Christian. Dianne was this kind of angel on earth. I love to hear stories of Dianne's impact and how friends and family continue to pay forward Dianne's blessings. I see the love for her and the witness of her faith.

In Our Actions

Giving our talents and money to charitable or nonprofit organizations is another way to be remembered. Finding a way for our earthly goods to improve the lives of others is an act of love, even with recognition to the person being remembered. Memories are how you are remembered for what you did; actions are what you can do. There are countless good causes justifiably in need that help others, but actions can also be within a family to improve the lives of loved ones. Christ teaches us to share love with our actions.

When I reflect on Dianne's life, I think about how she so often spent time helping others to have a better life and to find Christ is the answer. Dianne would want to be remembered by doing something that helps others. She provides me guidance by the way she lived her life. Dianne was always involved in some cause to help others. She also wanted to do more and would often talk about causes she wanted to help. The challenge, which charity? This is not an easy answer.

In Memorials

The world is full of memorials for us to reflect on our faith and inspire us to enjoy God's beauty of earth: A legacy of a statue, or window at church, something that reminds future generations of her acts of love. Our churches and schools have many examples of memorials that provide us inspiration and reflection points for our faith. A beautiful statue of Mary reminds us of her immaculate gift to us. A Cross reminds us that Christ died to provide for us eternal life. Stained-glass windows remind us inspirational stories from the Bible. Buildings donated for schools and hospitals remind us of faithful people. Often something as simple as a bench on a golf course that provides comfort reminds us of a loving son. The favorite park or a tree that provides comfort to future generations reminds us. I see these beautiful memorials that remind us of our faith.

Remembering Dianne

I search for answers by listening to everyone ideas and in prayer. Dianne's family will continue to remember and love her for eternity. So will her friends. I am not sure if Dianne's answer would be a bench, or a statue, or a stained glass window. I do have a couple of sound bites to consider. Dianne and I were once at Mass in a Las Vegas church, and I commented on the beautiful stained-glass windows and wondered who the people were that had their name on the window. I suggested that maybe we should donate something similar someday and have a plaque place on it. She scowled at me saying, "Why would you do that? You have better things you can use your money for". On another occasion I commented that I thought it would be nice to buy something for the church that we could look at and remember that we donated that. She said, "Don't use your money like that."

I believe that Dianne did not want to be remembered on earth, she wanted to be remembered for all eternity in heaven. She showed us how by blessing others with charity and compassion on earth is how we can share Christ's love and help us be remembered in heaven. We can honor Dianne by helping others find comfort and Christ's love. I know this is what she would tell us. that is what she would ask us to do. Sharing Dianne's extraordinary journey of serving others while suffering the challenges of cancer helps us honor her and help others.

We remember Dianne by continuing her devotion to helping others with selfless acts. We can honor Dianne with contributions to groups she helped while she was living. I hope something can provide others the same feelings as if Dianne was there giving them a hug of love and hope.

We organized scholarship endowment funds at Grand Island Central Catholic and Pius High School. These funds will award scholarships to students demonstrating similar faith, charity, and compassion as Dianne. We also organized a fund at the Heartland Cancer Foundation to assist cancer patients with expenses during chemo treatments. I pray these are how she would want to be remembered. Dianne inspires all of us to volunteer more and to not let our left hand know what our right hand is doing. I think she would scold me some because I put her name on endowment funds. But I want these funds to reflect her faith and the way she lived.

2. What Should I Do with Your Stuff?

Dianne never really placed value on objects like books, clothing, jewelry, shoes, or purses. We referred to it as "stuff." But I was surprised by how much stuff she had when she passed away. Only a few items were earmarked for special people, but the rest was up for grabs. We did not discuss what to do with this stuff. The only sound bites I have to consider again are very tactical. Dianne and I started cleaning out our storage of stuff we collected over the thirty-seven years of marriage. Dianne reflected on a shirt she saved that was her grandfather's and provided her special memories of her childhood. But she was quick to point out how our daughters would look at it and rightfully throw it away.

The complexity is most often in the value of this stuff. For example, Dianne had some coins she collected that included two silver dollars. To Dianne, these silver dollars have great sentimental value. One was a gift from her grandfather who she adored and the other was a gift from her Godmother, I think for her first communion. Anyone else would see silver dollars now without the sentiment that passed away with Dianne. Even if I pass them onto the next generation, the sentiment will not be the same. I could give one to each daughter, easily. But my banker sister-in-law did some quick research and determined that one was worth about $600 and the other about $60. This is especially true of some of Dianne's stuff—some things have little monetary value and others are very expensive. How do you "split them up"? and also how do you avoid donating them and someday have someone pay $10 for a $2,500 necklace?

Her jewelry is the first challenge. All the blue Tiffany boxes from thirty-seven years of marriage plus so many other gifts. The jewelry she collected was incredible. two daughters the easy answer is to give it to them. Pass the burden. Dianne did have two wedding bands named "Julie" and "Annie." She always wanted these to go to our daughters. That was easy. I also bought her a "Holly" ring that she wore for our granddaughter.

Many suggestions included splitting the remaining jewelry between family or donating or selling it. I agree I can donate most of the less expensive items and store the rest in a safe deposit box for future gifts. I wish we discussed this before she passed away because I do not know what really was special to her. My guess is the jewelry she wore all the time, so I shared many of these items with her close friends as a memory for them.

I refer to it as stuff and say that Dianne didn't place much sentiment in it, but I was also shocked by some of the sentimental items we found. For example, we found Dianne's POW bracelet from high school. We looked the soldier up and found out he was released after the Vietnam War and died several years ago. I pray for guidance on this stuff.

Shoes and purses are the next big group of stuff. I boxed up her boots, shoes, and purses in six containers! Dianne loved expensive shoes and purses. What should I do? Of course, none of her sisters, our daughters, or nieces are the same shoe size. We are humored by the thought our grandchildren might grow into the shoes. I only retained the expensive shoes and purses and donated the rest.

Clothing was easy. I donated most of her daily clothes. Our daughters and her sisters did pull out many of the clothes that fit and helped me store away the remaining expensive clothing. My guess is this also will be donated once everyone decides they do not want any more.

Shoes, purses, and clothing are very time sensitive from a fashion and a label perspective. So value again is a challenge. I can appreciate why people struggle with this challenge after their loved one dies. I can understand why some may wait years or even leave it for the next generation to resolve.

A friend recommended I have many of the items appraised, which will provide some guidance. Without her guidance I think this is the best approach to deciding what to donate: I recommend you create an inventory of the things that matter and then look at the remainder as stuff. Donate it or sell it, because my memories in the future of Dianne are about Dianne, not her stuff.

As I have shared these thoughts, I had the good fortune of many people sharing their similar experiences. As I was sharing this one night with a group, one young man told us of his struggle. He explained his mother was dying of cancer and his brothers and sisters were already fighting over her stuff. Another person reflected on how his mother passed away five years ago and his father had yet to open her closet or move any of her things. Our good friend shared a story of the struggle within his family. When his mother passed away her sister explained why she was mad at her for over thirty years. He shared his sorrow in learning the reason for the struggle was unnecessary because of a misunderstanding about who actually had the item. I learned so many stories of families in struggle over what to do with their loved one's stuff—who gets what and what is fair. I hear these stories of family struggles every time I share these conversations and wonder how a simple conversation could better honor our loved one with what to do with their stuff.

Dianne would tell us it's just stuff and could be more valuable to someone in need or hunger than left in a box for another generation to deal with. I also believe our loved one would donate or sell it rather than create conflict in a family. I do think we need to remember how we can honor our loved ones by how we treat their stuff with love and dignity. Also, this is a good example of an act of love you can do to help your loved one cope with their grieving. The actions of taking care of your stuff will gives them a guidance on how to honor you.

It's just stuff.

3. Where is ...

Many marriages are two people in love who share their lives but not everything is intermingled. Separate finances, vacations, friends are not unusual. However, there are some marriages where two people are so intertwined that they share one soul. They are so interlocked by Christ as one that they trust and commit to a true partnership. We depend on each other to take care of certain responsibilities. These responsibilities become how we share love for one another. We rarely strayed across the line questioning how the other did these responsibilities. Dianne and I had a marriage that grew into one soul with each of us taking care of our responsibilities without need for recognition. Dianne managed inside the house, and I was responsible for everything else. It was her kitchen, her way of shopping, cooking, cleaning, and paying our bills. Dianne's domain was also our faith, friends, and future. Dianne had great command of these responsibilities, but in her way. I know we would do these responsibilities completely differently.

Earlier in our marriage, everyone learned that Dianne would prepare for me what I would wear to work each day. I would laugh with our friends if they questioned my tie or shirt because I just wore whatever she decided. To an outside observer this may seem lazy on my part, but it really had to do with her laundry status. She knew what was clean and what she needed to clean for me each week. She would even pack my suitcase when I traveled; rarely did I know what was in it until I was at the hotel. Dianne organized everything in the house, including my clothes. I was always lost in my own closet and dresser because I grew up with only one drawer and everything I owned was in it. I was always asking her where things were. It just became part of our marriage and love. One Christmas we decided to spend our money on dry cleaning so she didn't have to iron every day. That was a big deal. Later Christmas presents included a housecleaner coming every few weeks and window washers.

Dianne also had her system for the kitchen. I would find myself standing in the kitchen asking where to find a dish; the organization of the kitchen never made sense to me. But it was her domain, so I left it alone. Later when she was sick and I needed to cook for her, she still would instruct me, even though I had figured her system out. It was still her domain.

Dianne also had a system for paying our bills. I never really understood it until after she passed away and I was organizing the process. Dianne always knew where she had put everything; just don't start opening cabinets or drawers looking. It will not make sense to anyone else. But it worked very well for her.

This sets up the third conversation. Where do I find ...? I am still finding pockets of statements, receipts, and papers months after she passed away. I have yet to find the life insurance policy. I was concerned because of the funeral expenses but laughed at God's sense of humor when at Dianne's funeral a gentleman I had not seen in decades come up to me and told me he had started the insurance paperwork. I have found most of the prior year's tax paperwork, but not all of this year's yet. I do not know all the passwords to the online accounts we shared.

I do not think we have a safe deposit box anymore only because I haven't found a key yet and I haven't received a bill. I know we had one years ago, but I am guessing she closed it.

I learned in our partnership these were her domains, and I should not try to interfere with her system. But now I am faced with trying to find these answers. This was a bigger challenge just after she passed away when there was an urgency to find certain documents. I would have better peace of mind if I knew where I could find things before she passed away.

I am not sure how I would share this with Dianne. Because the list is constantly changing, I do not worry about the little stuff. Creating a will helps with the "big stuff." It also helps identify the assets of value, but so much of our daily routine is not "big stuff." I think a simple checklist would help prepare for when one of you will be alone:

1. Get a will.
2. Create a financial statement annually of all accounts and values. Include access codes.
3. Do an insurance walk through the house. Are all legal and financial documents in a common location? Photograph locations of important stuff.
4. Point out items that you want to pass on to who and why.

I hear many other valuable suggestions but the key is communication.

4. What about Our Dreams?

Dianne and I never really had a bucket list. We did have many things we planned to do together—remodeling projects, new furniture, traveling the world, and many more, like finding new interests or hobbies we wanted in the future.

The best analogy for this conversation I think is peanut butter. I love chunky peanut butter, but for thirty-seven years we always had smooth. Why? Because it would melt evenly into Dianne's toast. Now that she is in heaven, I can make the change. Should I, can I, will I? This is a complex conversation because it impacts so many decisions and plans that we had that now are just mine. Do

I stay in our home and continue our remodeling plans or move? I do have one sound bite from Dianne to consider. One night a few months before she passed away I asked her what she would do if I died. Immediately she said she would get a dog and move into a townhouse. I was startled to learn she already had it thought out. I asked if she planned to bury me first. She laughed, saying she would after she bought the dog. I knew where I stood.

I always said I wanted to live in Maui. She said she would come and visit me if I moved. I don't think she liked my dream, and she may be right. I always enjoyed our conversations about the future but never really considered what if she died first. Even when she was very ill, I refused to let myself think about it because of guilt. She was full of hope, and I wanted to believe; I did believe.

Dianne always provided me the best and most loving opinion for me. She knew what was best for me even when I did not recognize it. I think this is the reason why I wish for this conversation. I give my life to Christ to guide me now because I do not have Dianne to gently lead me to my dreams.

I believe we need to discuss our dreams and encourage our loved one. Change is good and we should remind each other to change and not feel guilty.

5. A Long Hug and Kiss

This is about love. This is about how much I miss her. This is not about sex but the intimacy that comes from our daily kisses and hugs. I have many great memories, but I would love another hug. This is a reminder of Dianne's approach to life: to enjoy every day by finding time to share your love with the people close to you. This is not a threat but a reflection on how you can improve your soul by sharing your love by praying together holding hands.

For the last few years of her life she was in so much pain that even a hug was difficult. I was always so full of amazement and love when I watched people hug her and she would respond with so much kindness and love because I knew how much it physically hurt her every time. But she never would push people away because she knew what it meant to them. This is how much Dianne loved life and how she tried to make others feel good.

In the last month of her life I was lifting her from her chair to a transport as needed. She reached a point where should could not walk, or stand. I would usually have her put her arms around my neck and then lift her up. I learned later from hospice I was doing it completely wrong. But on a few occasions I would accuse her of making a pass at me and she would smile and said I would know it if she really was making a pass. We laughed a lot about how out of shape as I struggled to move her, and while she never complained, she poked fun. Her expression of love was in these moments as we worked together to take care of her. I would love to hug her again and share that moment of love holding hands and sharing in our Lord's Prayer.

I am often asked, do I remember the last kiss or hug? No. But I do remember with joy the thousands of times we did. I believe that no one moment can represent a lifetime of love. This is how I know Christ is comforting me. I hear it in my thoughts of Dianne, my memories, and especially when I pray for her.

I miss her and pray for her every day. I pray I will be in heaven with her someday.

Summary

So, I pray these conversations will bring you joy and more love because you will lessen the burden on your loved one once you pass away. Do not be afraid to talk about what if you die because you will die and leave your loved ones to deal with many burdens. Consider these conversations an act of love, not fear. I do not suggest you plan out your own funeral, decide the music, and write the eulogy. Show your loved ones how you want their life to be once you pass away. Christ gives you forgiveness and the promise of eternal life in heaven if you believe. These conversations will make your loved ones mourn your loss less by focusing on your intentions and the memories of your love.

God bless you.

Peace Be with You

I pray Dianne's journey helps you as much as writing her story helps me. Writing these reflections helps me find peace. We are never prepared for this journey for our loved ones. Dianne and I learned how to laugh at our fears and her challenges. Dianne changed the rules about how we considered treatments. Every week for the last two years she was in treatment at the cancer center or a hospital. She changed it to seem normal so everyone would not feel sorry constantly for her. What a gift.

Dianne and I share a single soul. Our soul is with her in heaven and with me on earth. Although we are not physically together and I lack signs of her, I know she is with me in our soul. Whenever I feel I am alone, I pray a rosary for Dianne. In the prayers I feel our soul and become filled with joy. When I am full of guilt and grief, I go to the cemetery to pray a rosary. I feel her love.

Here are some final lessons:

Be what you do, not what happens to you.

Dianne did not consider cancer a burden. She didn't want to have cancer, but her faith and trust led her to see the cancer as part of

God's plan for her. I think that is why she didn't ever complain. I heard her often tell people her cancer was nothing compared to the burdens of others. She was quick to point to parents with a lifelong commitment to care for a child in need. She admired people who cared for a husband after a tragic accident paralyzed him. I remember several of these examples of people she believed had a greater burden.

Live in the moment.

Consider today as your last day on earth: what would you do? Make a list and post it on your bathroom mirror so you look at it every morning. You will find your list will not include fears, frustrations, or anger. It should be full of good memories. Then start doing the things on the list each day and watch your worries and stress go away. I believe Dianne did not fear death; she just didn't want to die. She prayed she would go to heaven but she also wanted to spend more time on earth sharing Christ's love. She never showed any fear of death during her last weeks on earth. She didn't talk about dying because she often reminded us to not waste time worrying about the future. Enjoy the day. This is how she lived her life even during the final weeks.

Find peace.

Know you are loved by God and our departed loved ones. Love does not go away; only their physical presence. Dianne is with me as much today as when she was alive. Just because I cannot hug her does not mean I don't feel her love. I do miss her wisdom and wit. I trust my memories of her will keep me doing the right thing until I join her in heaven.

Let your faith shine.

Do not "hide it under a basket." Thank God for his blessings especially at meal time. I am always amazed at waiters and waitresses who will pause and pray with me when I dine. I love the smile on a stranger's face when I say "God bless you." Dianne showed us how to increase your happiness by sharing your faith. Be a faith warrior.

Find joy.

I pray you find joy in charity and compassion by helping someone in need. We are all blessed with the joy from family and friends when we let it happen. Christ says to love our neighbor, and this is a beautiful way to share your love. I love the easy random acts of kindness, liking buying the coffee for the car behind you at the drive-thru. Consider taking a case of water to the homeless shelter or a blanket. These are easy actions that take very little time and will create joy for another soul. Angels are all around us even among the homeless. Joy is easy to find when you help another before yourself.

Be a blessing.

Dianne always found a way to help you smile and know that Christ loves you. Find a way you can be a blessing to others continuing her legacy. Each blessing you share is a gift for God.

Be not afraid.

God is with you always and also our departed loved ones, in our thoughts and in our heart. May your heart overflow with God's love. Be angelic.

God bless you.